Kelli—
You got me...
thanks for your support!
H.—

Patriarch

MY EXTRAORDINARY JOURNEY
FROM MAN TO GENTLEMAN

A Memoir in Essays

H.L. SUDLER

ARCHER PUBLISHING
WASHINGTON, D.C.

ARCHER

Copyright ©2012 by H.L. Sudler

Library of Congress Control Number
2012902481

Archer Publishing ISBN
978-09848460-09

For information regarding special discounts for bulk purchases, please contact Archer Publishing Sales at business@archermedianetworks.com.

Archer Publishing can bring this author to your live event. For more information, follow @HLSudler on Twitter.

Printed in the United States of America

10 9 8 7 6 5 4 3 2 1

Front cover photograph by Giovanni Rinaldi
Back cover photograph by Robert Dodge

A number of the essays in this collection have appeared elsewhere, some in a slightly different form: "Ballad of the Gentleman" in Man to Gentleman, "The Acceptance Speech" in Nuance Magazine, "Yesterdays and Tomorrows" in the anthology Mighty Real: An Anthology of African American Same Gender Loving Writing, "From Here to Eternity" in the anthology Spirited: Affirming the Soul and Black Gay/Lesbian Identity, "Time Stood Still" in the Rehoboth Beach Gayzette, and "Patriarch" in Man to Gentleman.

2

DEDICATION

To my father Louis Lyles, Sr.:
For your patience with me during your life,
for the lessons I learned from you after your death.
I see things much more clearly now, as I suspect you knew I would.
-Junior

ACKNOWLEDGEMENTS

WHILE GRATITUDE appears to come these days all too seldom or insincerely, I wish to express thanks to the many people who have made this publication a realization. It was never my intent to publish a memoir, but I extend deepest warmth to those that have assisted in its creation, including the previous editors and publishers of a number of essays included in this book. Those individuals include Lisa Moore and G. Winston James, Frank Reynolds and Carol Fezuk, as well as R. Bryant Smith and Gregory Kompes, and the *Nuance Magazine* editorial team that worked with me on my first essay *The Acceptance Speech* back in 1994. I would be remiss if I did not thank editors Carol Taylor and Molly Gray for assisting me in polishing these collected essays, Robert Dodge for his photographic genius, Arlene Bernstein, Delores Orr, Helene Del Ricci, and Charles Cox for literary guidance through the years, and my network of supporters, mentors, advisors, and family. To my brother and sisters, my dearest friends Roger Sucharski, Lee Walker, Bob Witeck, Jim Villa, my DLP Brothers, and countless friends all across the globe and all through the years: my life was never always easy, but it has been made more special by your light. Finally: many, many thanks to Dana Mallory, who was there seemingly from the very beginning. And *gracias, mi amor* to Geovanny Mendez: who is always there now.

H.L. SUDLER
PATRIARCH

H.L. SUDLER was born and raised in Philadelphia, Pennsylvania and is the recipient of a PATHS Humanitarian Writing Award. He has served as publisher of *Café Magazine*, editor of the *Rehoboth Beach Gayzette*, as well as a contributing writer for numerous anthologies and such publications as *Page & Author*, *Nuance Magazine*, *Au Courant Magazine*, and the *Lambda Book Report*. He lives in Washington, D.C.

CONTENTS

BY THREE methods we may learn wisdom: first, by reflection, which is noblest; second, by imitation, which is easiest; and third by experience, which is the bitterest.

–Confucius

OF THOSE armies so rapid, so wondrous, what saw you to tell us?
What stays with you latest and deepest? Of curious panics,
Of hard-fought engagements or sieges tremendous, what deepest remains?

The Wound Dresser
–Walt Whitman

Patriarch

essays

INTRODUCTION

MY NAME is H.L. Sudler. I am a walking contradiction. I always have been, really. Born equal parts of diverse parents, my life was and remains a constant struggle between the good and bad parts of each. My mother: Puerto Rican, adopted, crafty both in nature and spirit, is also extremely intelligent, talented, complex, volatile, formidable, untrustworthy, duplicitous, and heinous. My father: born in Union, South Carolina and one of six children, was an alcoholic, a simple man, well-loved by friends and family, a hard worker; also volatile, stubborn, a tale spinner, and habitually depressed.

I grew up in Philadelphia, Pennsylvania no more tragically than any other child who is the product of a broken home. I am the eldest of four: two boys and two girls. My earliest childhood memory is of me in a crib watching my father arguing furiously with my mother—an omen to our future family dynamics. By the time I was 5 years old my parents were separated and by the time I was 8 years old they were divorced. My father remarried quickly and had two daughters by that union. My brother and I remained with my mother.

The battleground that was to be my childhood, which definitively shaped me into who I am today, was fatherless and

9

filled with abuses both mental and physical. At the age of 7, my mother made me watch *The Exorcist* over and over as a punishment for something trivial. I do not think I'll ever recover from that betrayal. She often slapped, punched, and beat me for very little or no reason at all until I left home for college. She has thrown hot tea thrown on me, slapped me on the head with a stack of hardcover books, and spit in my face.

She humiliated me in front of friends, family members, or people that I did not know or barely knew. She called me a fag, told me that I was weak and stupid, and that I, like my father, laughed too much, and was too friendly with people. At 16, she made me strip nude in the living room—in front of my brother—for an impromptu, pointless and fruitless drug search. My brother told me that he was my mother's favorite son because that is what she had told him. Later, my mother vindictively prevented anyone in my family from attending my high school graduation, despite the fact that I received a full four-year scholarship to Temple University, among other honors. She did, however, manage to cash a check for a book scholarship awarded to me for winning a writing contest. I never saw any of that money, nor any of the other money she stole from me. Nor my childhood, of which I also felt I had been robbed. It has always been my belief that the constant abuse she inflicted upon me was a misguided attempt at attacking my father. And that every time she looked at me she saw a piece of him and felt burning inside of her all the unresolved issues the two of them

10

shared.

The twenty essays in this book are stories about my life. Some of them are harsh; all of them are filled with lessons I've learned, some easily, some not so much. They are meant to be cathartic—a way of coming to terms with many of the less-than-pleasant events that have hallmarked my life, a way of reminding myself of what is important. They are also meant to be inspirational and empowering, for we've all had, at one time or another, issues to overcome in the process of growing. That's life and the business of living. For instance, in *Service Man* and *Lucky Thirteen* I recount a dark period in my early teens and the resources that helped me to develop into a responsible young man. Later in life when I sought to escape other demons, my understanding of faith's true power became my salvation, as you'll read in *The One That Got Away* and *From Here to Eternity*. In *Mortality* and *Swimming Toward the Sun* I find inspiration and the drive to attain my goals. In *Dangerous Ground, But Not For Me* and *You Say You Want a Revolution* I learn from lessons not necessarily my own.

The majority of my memories and recollections involve family and friends and the lessons I learned and the wisdom I gained from them. In *Dove*, I recount the relationship with my first love and how I subjected her to nearly insurmountable pain. In *Yesterdays and Tomorrows*, I recall three childhood friends who each became a casualty of AIDS in the early years of the disease—and then were quickly forgotten by nearly everyone

11

who knew them. In *The Brotherhood*, my involvement with a fraternity explores how I learned to be a team player despite having become a very mistrustful person. Other essays like *Closer* and *The Acceptance Speech* reveal the often-rocky relationship I shared with my father and the pride I now feel at being his son. *Missing You Missing Me* is an open letter to my brother regarding our early years together, and in *Her* I share my advice on how to survive an abusive childhood that could easily define your very existence. The pieces that bookend this collection, *Ballad of the Gentleman* and *Patriarch*, serve as a celebration of life and stress the value and responsibility of passing lessons learned on to others, to younger generations, and to those who need them. To my astonishment, the lifelong experience of learning and giving has revealed to me a greater man inside, the gentleman I've become, and the patriarch I was meant to be.

PART ONE

REAR VIEW VISION

BALLAD OF
THE GENTLEMAN

As I WAS INTRODUCED as "Our distinguished guest Mr. Sudler" I thought of a photograph of my mother and father that I have hanging in my living room. It was taken the year I was born and in it my father, young and very handsome, looks dashing in a tuxedo. I thought of him and our relationship as I stood in front of a classroom of fifty young men, aged between 16 and 18, whose eyes were filled with curiosity, mistrust, anger and boredom. The relationship I had with my father was never easy, even up to his dying day, but now more than ever there is buried inside of me a deep-seeded love and respect for him. Being a young father of four willful and intelligent children and a borderline alcoholic in a difficult marriage could not have been easy on him. As I looked out at the audience it struck me how dumbfounded all these young men seemed, as if no one had spoken to them about the logistics of being a man or how hard or tricky it is. Yet, here I am called in to inform them of just that, on how to make a success of themselves against the odds— against even themselves—and how to be what they see me as today, an accomplished and well-rounded gentleman.

Let's go back to the spring of 2006 when I was working in the AOL Legal Department. I was assigned two young men from high schools in the area to trail me during Job Shadow Day. Jason, the young black male, was from a prestigious high school in Northern Virginia who was interested in a career in investment banking. Mark, the young white male, was from a vocational high school in a rural suburb in Virginia and was unclear about his career path. As I spoke with them, I quickly realized how different they were from each other. Jason was ambitious, determined and clear-minded about the path he wished to travel. I believe he was being raised by a single mother who had a strong influence in his life. Mark was more laid back. He smiled a lot but I could tell he was insecure. I got the impression his insecurity had a lot to do with the fact that Jason was intelligent and more vocal and secure about himself and his future than Mark.

I talked with them about the law—a subject that interested neither—and then I stopped, realizing I was discussing the wrong topic. I recalled a saying from the Bible: if you give a man a fish you feed him for one day but if you teach him *how* to fish you'll feed him for a lifetime. I quickly changed the subject to what they believed was the secret of my success, which was

15

how put-together I appeared to them: my expensive suit, my manners, my clean and organized office, and how comfortable I was in my own skin and surroundings.

I asked them about their home lives. Jason referenced only his mother as an influence in his life; while Mark was sketchy about his relationship with his family, which gave me the impression he may have had a crowded house and was left to fend for himself. Since they were both juniors we discussed schooling and where they were in the application process for higher education. Not only had they not done any work in this area, neither had discussed it with their parents or guidance counselors. Immediately, I gave each of them pen and paper and instructed them to start taking notes. I advised them on conversations they should have, people to contact, where to get scholarship money and loans, the importance of working while in college, the importance of establishing their own bank accounts and so on.

I moved on from schooling to getting their first job, how to put together a resume, how to behave on the job, what to wear, and then to striking out on their own, girlfriends (or boyfriends), and some basic principles of living. When it was time for them to go, they fervently asked for my card and promised to keep in touch. However, it was only Mark who contacted me. I now stood before him and his class because I'd been invited to address fifty young men at the vocational school he attended.

I WAS BORN AND raised in Philadelphia, Pennsylvania. I grew up in a broken home and have a brother and two sisters, all younger. I matured mostly on my own, learning for myself everything from how to pay bills to housekeeping, from building manners to building wealth, and from cooking and entertaining to daily exercise and proper hygiene. All this led me to believe that parents fall out of touch with their children after a certain age and what teenagers discover as they age into adults is mostly by chance, accident and/or observation.

After Job Shadow Day, Mark told his teachers how impressed he was by what I'd told him and they, both female, invited me to speak to two of their classes. They'd told me that while they had made a connection with the young women of the school with respect to their futures, they had not had as much success with the young men. They had seen what I also witnessed: a general lack of gentlemen in the world, of young men with ideas and opinions and direction in their lives, of young men who are responsible, ambitious and driven. But beyond that were issues ranging from wardrobe to hygiene, self-preservation, money, diction, manners, sex, work, self-respect, which are independent of race or class and vary from man to man, resulting in an uneven balance of maturity across the board.

It is this lack of direction and responsibility that robs today's young men of drive, purpose, and commitment, among other parts of their character. This problem is not exclusive to young men; I also see it in older men and in men of all races. I see it in

17

men of all socio-economic groups as well as in various intellectual, regional, religious, and sexual groups. It is everywhere and has the potential to detrimentally affect current and future generations. It is in response to this deficiency that I decided to speak to Mark's class, and to write this book.

To be fair, being a man is not easy, certainly not as easy as some people believe. Contrary to popular belief, being a man is not about putting just your pants on one leg at a time, throwing on shoes and a shirt and running your fingers through your hair; it has always involved so much more, but particularly now in an age where there is constant societal debate over what constitutes acceptable male self-expression.

Can a man be true to his race and heritage and still be successful without looking like either a rebel or a sellout? Can he be openly gay? What if he is more artistic than intellectual? What if he's poor? How does his body affect his self-image? How does he relate to other men? How does he relate to women? What if some of his aspirations have not been fulfilled? Is he too old to turn his life around, to find love? Is there comparative happiness? What if he has health issues that burden him? What if he is a father or guardian? And if he has everything he's always wanted—what next? Why is so much expected out of him simply because he is a man?

I laid it out for these fifty young men at Mark's school, as much as I could. Predictably, there was just not enough time—a little more than an hour—to tell them what they really needed to know to get them through the first years on their own after high school. And that was nothing compared to what they needed to know in the grand scheme of being a man. There are so many years of life ahead of them. So many twists and turns, tricky questions, impossible scenarios, and difficult choices to make. Most of what I discussed was procedural—issues involving school, first jobs, money, and independence from family—mixed with my philosophy on healthy living. Regardless, the talk was good and ended well with most of them coming up to shake my hand and ask for my card. Still, the whole thing left me with a sense of incompletion, as if I had failed as a parent because I didn't get to even half of what it really takes to be a man.

THE QUESTION IS: WHAT would you tell a young man–all men in fact–if you had to describe what they fundamentally needed to know about being a mature and responsible man? Being a gentleman takes finesse, but is a very attainable goal. If you could provide men everywhere with information that would do more than warn them about life's ups and downs, that would transform them into more than just mere men, that would arm them with tools for a full and successful road of life ahead, what would you tell them?

Patriarch is about all the things I have learned either the hard way or by reading, from advice, by example or simply good fortune. These stories encompass and outline what I've learned from my mentors, men *and women* I've admired, and my friends

19

and family. I have bent and stretched and shaped every day from these lessons into a man I am proud to be. And in the course of this work I have become a gentleman.

I recall my father's funeral and standing before all his friends and family. The large church was nearly filled; so many people had known him. They all came to me and shook my hand, saying that my father was a good man, that he spoke often of me, that he was proud. Later that night in bed, exhausted but sleepless, I thought that if I had that many people at my funeral who thought so well of me I would die half the man he was. If my father were alive today I would tell him to keep his head above water and swim! I would tell him the same thing I'd tell any man: to breathe and rely on his faith, to dig deep for strength, to reach out for help, to stop living as if getting from day to day is all he is capable of doing. I would tell him to search for what makes him special, for what makes him happy, and for what makes him an individual. I would tell him that dreaming is never off limits, to embrace his personal evolution, and to embrace the gentleman he was born to be. I would tell him to swim, swim, swim.

SERVICE MAN

PLAINLY PUT, MY relationship with my mother is not good and never will be. But out of a painful, trying and often miserable childhood, an extraordinary part of my life was born: the beginning of an era of service that remains a source of pride. In all likelihood, my mother is unaware that she created in me a love of service at an early age. The summer between my thirteenth and fourteenth birthdays was a time of awakening for me. It was the summer in which the divide between my mother and I irreversibly widened. It was the summer I would embark upon my love affair with literature that, in hindsight, served as a haven from the gritty reality that was my life. It was when I realized I would never share a loving and meaningful relationship with the woman who gave birth to me. It was also the time I realized my perspective on life was changing; and that with each day I was becoming a different, more evolved person heading unwaveringly into the uncharted terrain of manhood. I was walking through a minefield of adult dilemmas, where all decision-making would rest squarely with me. I would have the final word on the direction my life would take–a very scary proposition for a young adult—for it was clear that there would be no parent I could go to for advice. I knew that not all my choices would be the right ones, and that they would be weighted with the threat of heavy consequence. Because of that summer every decision I have made is the result of a deep and deliberate contemplation.

Of those decisions, one turned out to be more extraordinary and lasting than any other in my life. Between my thirteenth and fourteenth birthdays, my mother decided to get me out of the house by any means possible. She demanded that I find a summer job, regardless of my being below the legal working age for a teenager. This tasked me with finding a way to occupy my days from the early hours of the morning to mid-evening. Up until that point I usually spent most summer days in my room quietly but ravenously devouring books, so it was by luck that I managed to see an ad in a weekly Philadelphia alternative newspaper, the now defunct *Welcomat*, looking for volunteers or candy stripers for Metropolitan Hospital, which sat between Chinatown and Old City, only blocks from where I lived in Society Hill.

The term candy striper is said to have originated at New Jersey's East Orange General Hospital in 1944 and referred to the red and white (peppermint) striped uniforms young female volunteers wore. While candy stripers were very popular in the following decades and usually reserved for ages thirteen through eighteen, the term has largely been retired in lieu of the less colorful label VOLUNTEER. I was one of the few males in the overwhelming majority of female candy stripers. Regardless of sex, the job was ideal for a young teen and called for only very basic duties and responsibilities. I ran the mail cart in the mornings, the donated magazine and book trolley in the afternoons, and filled in at the information booth at lunch. I assisted recovering patients on their daily walks, I filed, ran errands for hospital personnel, and entered data for various departments. For three years I was a member of the Metropolitan Hospital candy striper program, spending the final two years in the cardiology unit gathering invaluable office experience.

One of my more memorable moments as a striper was after a Fourth of July car accident on the Benjamin Franklin Bridge that killed a number of people, but left one woman alive and clinging dearly for life. She seemed to be in her early thirties, blonde, and terribly bruised and battered by the wreck. She spent a number of days in and out of consciousness and was understandably severely depressed after she awoke, having lost loved ones in the crash. It was clear her life would never be the same ever again. One day I was on my afternoon run and

23

entered her room to offer her a *People* magazine or a Danielle Steele novel—I had heard of her and her story, but had never spoken with her. She was perched at the room's window, which of all awful ironies provided a view of the bridge where the accident had occurred. Her eyes were vacant and red from crying, and her face was etched with pain. I was young and ignorant and had no idea what to say to one experiencing such a loss. Then I realized that was the point. I was not there to talk. I was there to listen and provide support. After a moment of silence, she started speaking absently about the accident, how one car crossed over from the opposing lane into hers, how the headlights blinded her against the night, how the car struck hers head on, and how quickly she heard the impact and the sound of crushing metal and breaking glass. She then wept long and silently, her head bent low as I held her hand and rubbed her back. I stayed with her until she composed herself and crawled back into bed, retreating from the world, unable to escape that horrible memory. In all my years I have never forgotten how hurt she was or stopped wishing that my visit had comforted her in some way.

From that day, I made a silent commitment to service. I honored my commitment during my first year at university when I enrolled in a local government literacy program. After that, I volunteered in a program that trained adults for their G.E.D. examinations. Another year I joined a church volunteer program

24

that fed seniors. Later, I would volunteer regularly at Philadelphia's annual AIDS Walk, at Safeguards (passing out condoms and literature on safe sex), and at MANNA (selling pies to raise money for a meals-on-wheels program for those who were housebound). I have done clothing drives, coat drives, food drives, toy drives, drives for overseas military personnel, Salvation Army and United Way campaigns, disaster relief, community center revitalizations, book collections for children, and magazine collections for hospitals. I have belonged to programs that support individuals with AIDS, seniors, runaway and displaced teens, or those with disabilities. I have bagged food for underprivileged families and made countless monetary donations for various causes, including those championed by a good number of my friends, such as breast cancer research and awareness marketing, animal rescue and adoption, third world community education and famine relief, even funding for programs for female survivors of rape and domestic violence.

In the summer of 2008, I had the opportunity to serve in the gulf region of the United States that had been devastated by Hurricane Katrina in the summer of 2005. Katrina, the deadliest and most financially-destructive natural disaster in the history of North America, claimed more than 1,800 lives. Years after Katrina hit, many regions along the Gulf Coast remain abandoned and destroyed, with their citizens displaced. As part of an initiative sponsored by Time Warner, I was one of a

25

number of employees who assisted in building a computer lab for an elementary school in Pearlington, Mississippi that had been flooded to the roof. The hurricane had destroyed much of the town of Pearlington, and the residents were grateful for our presence and contribution.

A colleague and I traveled to New Orleans to see first-hand the city's lower ninth ward. It was as astonishing as it was heartbreaking. The New Orleans that I remembered from a visit years earlier was now barren, with neighborhoods completely deserted and in various stages of decline. Many houses were abandoned, the doors marked with a large X and the streets, for what appeared to be miles, were uncharacteristically desolate and lifeless. Even the French Quarter, normally a hub of music, people and activity was strangely silent as though awaiting an absolution that had already passed it by.

HERE IS WHAT I think, what I believe: there needs to be a collective return to service in our culture. Not exclusively in the face of disaster, but as a regular occurrence in our lives. There are too many communities in need, and far too many causes in peril without it. Unfortunately, it is usually crisis that spurs our sympathy and involvement, leaving a good number of causes to slip past public awareness. If we as a society incorporated service into our daily lives and treated it with the same importance as education or commerce, the world would benefit immeasurably.

26

A commitment to service should begin early. When an opportunity for service is presented at an early age, a generational commitment is born. Young people—with all their energy—need never be bored or left with idle hands. Service would provide them an excellent opportunity to develop skills, which they can list on their resumes. It gives them work experience, which comes in handy when they are looking for their first job. It introduces them to different types of people, many of whom will become their mentors or role models. Service also introduces them to the world around them and important inherent issues, while teaching them problem solving, how to think on their feet, and how to be proactive. These are skills that can never be learned too early in life.

For the rest of us, service should be part of our everyday living. The saying: Give back to your community implies that a community must first give you something before you offer it something back. I believe that we must give without any expectation. Give because someone in the world is in need. Give because it feels good. Give because it sets a good example. Give because the person or organization you help can assist someone else in need. Service in our everyday lives helps those programs and not-for-profit groups that work so hard to provide for those in need. And they do it with very little funding, overworked employees, and with little fanfare or recognition. We should offer our services and support to as many programs as possible during the course of our life. There are so many avenues, so many different ways to give. Something as simple as sweeping a road or picking up trash can make a big difference in your community. If you're good with your hands you can help build a playground, paint a church or clean a community center. If you love books or reading, you can teach someone to read, or read to children or seniors. If you are enthusiastic and love being with kids you can mentor or become a Big Brother or a Big Sister. Or do something as simple as donating food or clothing to those in need, finding homes for stray animals or fostering them until a home is found. Or if you've overcome adversity or addiction in your life, your experience and support can help others in recovery persevere.

The funny thing about life is that at any moment any one of us can find ourselves in need, by way of hurricane, fire, bad economy or just an awful twist of fate. It is sobering to find yourself on the bad side of misfortune. But nothing can make a bigger or lasting difference than an act of encouragement or the comfort of goodwill, while nothing glows quite brighter than the pride of service or the offering of fellowship.

THE ACCEPTANCE SPEECH

MY EARLIEST MEMORY of my father is of him arguing furiously with my mother. My father, handsome and barely over twenty, and my mother, not yet twenty, stood face to face tearing each other apart with words I could not understand. But what I did understand was their raw emotion, their naked anger and rage, which upsets me to this very day when I think back on it. I wondered how my parents, who were supposed to be in love, could snap feverishly at each other like wolves in a jungle. At that time I was a prisoner in my crib and I did what all babies do when they're upset. I cried loudly and angrily.

It was my mother who came to calm me. My father gritted his teeth, rolled his eyes and stormed from the room, punctuating his departure by slamming the door, the echo of which resonated for years in my memory and proved to be thoroughly prophetic on how discussions would often end between us. What I retained from that moment was very significant: an anger was born. Like a spark that blazes into an inferno, I became consumed by anger.

By the time I became an adult, everyone could see it but me. But angry at what or with whom? It took me a long time to realize that I was angry at the bitter arguments and fights and the long stints of silence and separations that hallmarked my relationship with my father for almost thirty years. But there was something more. I had been angry all those years since the confrontation he had with my mother, for that day when I witnessed them arguing from my crib marked a division in my family never to be fully repaired. It also set the stage for what was to become the drama of my family's relationships. There grew a wall between my mother and father; a wall between my mother and me (I later found out about her part in that argument and many others between them); and lastly, a wall between my father and myself. Add to that: after many years of skirting the issue, I finally broke down and admitted to being gay. As if everything else wrong between us was not enough.

ONCE UPON A TIME

MY MOTHER DIVORCED my father when I was still very young; her reason was his alcoholism. Their divorce could have been labeled brainwashing, because she turned us children against him without letting us hear his side of the story. The first seven years of my life hold very little memory of him. What I know of my father and his side of the family I gleaned from my mother and her tales about them. During those early ages of my approval-

30

seeking childhood I accepted whatever my mother had to say about him, which was mostly disparaging.

The next substantial memory I have of my father came when I was either 12 or 13. He arrived at my grandmother's house where my younger brother and I were staying for the weekend. He talked with my mother's mother for awhile (the two of them got along famously) before stopping to chat with my brother. Two-and-a-half years my junior, my brother Hasshi never really had a relationship with our father, he seemed to my younger brother almost a complete stranger. Nevertheless, they shared an animated conversation. But when my father came to speak to me all hell broke loose. Dipping into my deep well of anger, I spat forth the most hateful words a child could say to his parent. Like some demonic entity I let him have it. I called him irresponsible, pathetic, and an alcoholic. The truly amazing thing is that despite my ranting he did not strike me, and did not so much as raise his voice. Instead, he tried in vain to explain his side of the story—but I did not want to hear it. He even went so far as to offer me money, which I rejected. I was to be the victor of this confrontation, one in which he was nearly reduced to tears. I won, so I thought, and exited the room by slamming the door in his face. Literally.

GENTLEMAN'S AGREEMENT

ALL OF THE future confrontations between my father and I ended just as badly: winner takes all. And the older I became,

31

the less of a winner I was. Once we were at a family picnic and he flirted with my girlfriend Yolanda. He claimed that I didn't really want her and wouldn't know how to handle her even if I tried. There was another time when he accused me of touching my younger sister in a fashion that was not brotherly. And then there were those holiday events where he showed up, much to my chagrin, and he simply ignored me.

The times that truly hurt my feelings, however, were when he would dote on my cousins. His sister has three boys, all of whom are masculine and outgoing. He laughed with them, played with them, showed that he could be a good male role model. Of course I was jealous but also confused why he didn't treat me, his son, that way. What had gone wrong between us? How had we started off so badly? Deep down I had ached for my father's love and approval, but he never complimented or praised me.

As I watched him be loving and attentive to my cousins, I considered calling a truce between us. I wanted a gentleman's agreement that we would stop fighting and behave as a father and son. That chance came the more I investigated my father's side of the family. Most of what my mother had told me seemed far-fetched when I became reacquainted with them, so I threw out all earlier preconceptions about my father and his family and I asked him to teach me how to drive, which seemed a very good place to start. For the first few years we made baby steps toward creating a relationship: conversations here and there, a shared laugh, a beer together at times. That was until the gay issue came up, and the door slammed once again. This time in *my* face.

THE GAY ISSUE

I THINK ONE of the most hurtful things to happen to the average man is to find out that his son is gay. I do not fully understand why that is. Perhaps he feels that he has not parented correctly, or he feels that he has produced a dud or a deviant. When my father learned of my sexual orientation his eyes housed a look that, without words, spelled out the depths of his pain. I knew from the look he gave to me that he felt not only had his marriage to my mother been a failure but that the offspring from that marriage proved to be spoiled fruit. Like a battered spouse, his eyes expressed his grief and feeling of betrayal.

Blaming myself, I withdrew into my hard shell and he vacated back to my cousins. Soon after I came out to him, family functions became a sort of circus with sidelong looks and whispered conversations. Statements like: *Well, Lou, what can you do? You can't raise him all his life. I just hope he doesn't get the AIDS*, followed by giggles and snickering. I was embarrassed for him knowing that while they may have been laughing at me, they were also laughing at him. *Poor Lou. Couldn't keep a wife and his eldest son is a fag.*

33

Snowballing from bad to worse, I could not get any conversation out of him. If we were to attend the same function, he would no-show. Or if he was present, he reluctantly offered a mumbled salutation and went on his way. I tried to communicate with him; I really did. I wanted to apologize for embarrassing him. I did not wish to lose our momentum. I felt we were going somewhere and I did not believe–or wish to believe–that my being gay was that much of a big deal. I didn't want drama; I had experienced enough of that growing up with my mother. I also didn't want to believe that I was going to fall into that statistic of gay men who lose all or part of their family when they come out. So to my family's amusement, I tried. At family functions, they would wink to each other and smile and pat me on the shoulder when my father would ignore me.

Then one day I stopped. Like a room that fades to darkness when you turn out the light, my feelings for bridging a relationship were quickly shut off. I would no longer make a fool of myself. The door had been shut in my face and I decided to stop banging on it demanding to be let in. Instead I turned away and continued on with my life, without him.

THE LOVE LETTER

MANY YEARS LATER, I received a call informing me that my father was ill and in the hospital and that I should come see him. I did. He was in bad shape. Years of drinking had taken a toll

34

on his heart. I did my best to be the caring son. He did his best to be the ailing father. We were like actors, each deserving some award for coming so close to a topic of conversation without actually discussing it. There was so much baggage between us that I am amazed we were able to see each other through it. He hadn't spoken to me in many years so contact with him now was strange. We kept it up for a while after he was released: a word here, a word there, at family gatherings. And then he was in again–and again–to the hospital, with each stay more serious than the last, until finally the discussion of early retirement came up. I became concerned. I made an effort to repair our relationship, believing that time was of the essence; that I was going to lose him. We had been fighting for way too long, and he might go to his grave not knowing that I truly did love him.

My father wasn't an extraordinary man. He was a good and decent individual with simple pleasures. A hot meal, a cold beer and something on the television after a long day at work. Through some miraculous intervention of God, it finally sunk into my skull that my dad wasn't the president, or Superman, or an action hero. He was just my dad. I finally understood that this was who he was and that I should love and respect him for that. That life for him was not easy and never had been.

Retirement came up and to help him pass the long days at home I visited, brought him gifts, and discussed things he found important. And you know what? It worked. We clicked. We were too tired to fight anymore. Too old. We became loving and caring toward each other: shaking hands, laughing with one another. Then one day something wonderful happened, as if God had smiled upon me. As I was leaving from Thanksgiving dinner at my aunt's, he stopped me and pulled me down, to where he was sitting, and whispered: "I love you. No matter what you are. You take care of yourself." And then he hugged me.

On the way home, I was shocked to the point of tears. Never had I heard those words from his mouth. Never. I'll never know what inspired him to tell me he loved me. I assume what happened was that he finally found what I had found: acceptance. Each of us accepting the other as the person that he is, that he is always going to be. As father and son, as a gay man and a working Joe. As two people in love but who had a really hard time telling each other. Is this a love letter to my father? Of course it is. I gave this essay to him as a Father's Day gift. To let him see how much I care. To let him know that acceptance is a two-way street that no relationship can work without it. That I had found acceptance too. I gave this article to him so that he could pick it up any time and see, in black and white, how much I really do care. And that I have always longed to say to him this:

I love you, Dad.

Happy Father's Day.

YESTERDAYS
AND TOMORROWS

What have you learned from your life? What will you take with you when you die? Will it be all the lessons you have learned, all the pain you remember? Romances, milestones, regrets, eras?

SOMEHOW I ALWAYS manage to return in my head to the events that have hallmarked my life, steering it into a direction unforeseen, jarring me out of complacency or ignorance; an existence created as if I lived on a whole other plane than the rest of the world. I turn these thoughts over like pancakes on a griddle, flipping events this way and that, examining them, but always arriving at the same questions for which I have no absolute answer.

What have you learned from your life? What will you take with you when you die?

I ask myself these questions on my birthday, as I always ask myself these questions at what I believe to be the most reflective time of year. Since that date comes around in December, the same month as World AIDS Day, I always have cause to remember the three men I had come to know in my life, all at the same time, dead from AIDS—dead and buried, gone from the world, gone before I even knew they had the disease, gone, it seems, even from collective memory.

Lawrence Blakely, Laurence Gray, and Bernard Little were all friends of mine in high school—and let them be remembered here and now, for they are all forgotten. We spent three years together laughing, joking, studying, creating memories, but also growing as kids do, foraging into adulthood as if with blindfolds donned and hands outstretched. We held on to each other, relied on each other, fought and made up, not realizing the importance of our friendship, not realizing the importance of our bond as men, as African American men, as gay African American men.

Laurence Gray was my girlfriend's sidekick at that time. He was very short and lively with a wide, infectious smile and an equally contagious laugh. His face beamed and lit up a room, but he was also very emotional and would cry at the drop of a hat. He lived a terrible life at home, his family was poor and he was often hungry and no one wanted him. He became one of my best friends, as he was always at my girlfriend's side, keeping her laughing, keeping her company. I was dour and very serious then, as I am now, but he had the natural ability to make anyone laugh, even me.

He was partially responsible for me winning a student government campaign, handing out flyers, and making up posters. I helped him with his studies, shared my lunch with him, or gave him money to keep him fed during the day. We held a Secret Santa for our group of friends one Christmas and I remember him gifting my girlfriend a white stuffed bear that she adored. I remember him in a fight once, and I remember being shocked at how strong he was for a little guy, how much anger he carried with him—he was no taller than five feet, two inches. He was proud to be an Aquarius.

Bernard was a little taller. Make that a lot. Taller than my five feet, seven inches. But he was lanky and not terribly good-looking. If he had been given the opportunity to grow older, he might have grown into his looks and become handsome. Either way, he was a busybody, and what old-timers would call *a hoot*. He referred to himself as Millie and he would breeze through the school hallways, his lunch in a wrinkled plastic supermarket bag dangling from his wrist, his torn school bag held together by safety pins, his outfits shit brown and polyester, worn sometimes two or three times a week, smelling stale. He had grown up disadvantaged and pushed on his grandmother. You could tell in his eyes that he sensed his future had limited options and that he was living only for today.

He gravitated toward me like a dedicated puppy dog and we developed a strange friendship. He loved my bad boy attitude, that I was fearless, tough and direct. He was a confidant, even though we never discussed our common sexuality. Like me, he was a member of the school's drama club, and on breaks we would joke around and he would laugh gaily and without conscience. Everyone knew him—teachers, staff, nerds, jocks. Out of school he was considered a nobody, invisible. But in school he was a celebrity in our little high school soap opera; comic relief that reminded us that if someone like him could find laughter despite his circumstances, so could the rest of us. So we embraced him as much as we could.

Lawrence Blakely was a radically different story altogether. He was in each of my classes but he and I were not all that close. He was tall, husky, black as newly applied tar and just as shiny. Yet, for as large as he was he walked with dainty little steps, like a girl, as if he was worried he would disturb the universe with his presence. He spoke in a small nasally voice, his eyes distorted behind unflattering bifocals. His teeth were unnaturally white, and from time to time he emitted a laughter that was deep and throaty, as if to hint at the man he would become. A week before our senior graduation, Lawrence Blakely and Laurence Gray got into a fight in the chemistry lab–an epic battle not unlike David and Goliath. I was the school's student government vice-president at that time and knowing the fight could prevent them from participating in commencement ceremonies I tried to break them up. It turned out to be a huge mistake. The massive Lawrence Blakely attacked me and all three of us found ourselves in the principal's office with the threat of suspension over our heads.

Then there was graduation. Then they were dead.

After we left high school, I never saw or heard from Lawrence Blakely or Laurence Gray ever again, and saw Bernard Little only once. As I was walking down the street in downtown Philadelphia one day about five years after graduation, another friend from school (who was also black and gay) informed me that Bernard Little and Laurence Gray had died within a week of each other. The funerals had been two and three weeks prior. A little more than a year later, this same friend would tell me of Lawrence Blakely's death. Despite the fact that he had lost weight, shed his glasses and his timid gait and became a gym boy–fully evolved into the butterfly he was meant to be—he too succumbed quickly to the disease. All of their families had disowned them and they suffered and died for the most part alone.

I was so burned by this, so ashamed that I had immersed myself in college life and parties, that I was spurred to do something in their memory. I would not allow these men to rest in my brain as nothing more than fading tombstones in a cemetery. I began to volunteer at local Philadelphia AIDS charities. At ActionAIDS and For All Walks of Life, at MANNA and Safeguards, doing everything from selling pies to handing out condoms and literature at clubs. I attended fundraisers,

41

volunteered at AIDS walks and LGBT Pride festivals. I served as a Buddy to people suffering from HIV and AIDS and a mentor to others looking to serve.

The people I encountered at these organizations changed my life. They were angels, amazing one and all, each of them so different from the other, yet all of them bound together in grief and hope. My favorites were 67 year old Mister Jim, who volunteered in the memory of his beloved son, and the rough and tough Jimmy O., as young and handsome as he was, was a man who never got over losing the love of his life, whose grief cloaked him like a scent, who volunteered courageously, and seemingly tirelessly. The soldiers at these organizations were like a secret society working diligently for people they had lost, and for people they knew who were suffering from the disease, for people they did not know at all: men, women, gay, straight, transgendered, young, old, black, White, Latino, Asian. The hours were long and there was always so much to do, but we existed as a family unto ourselves and they welcomed me with open arms.

I was ashamed of my ignorance–for that is the only word that aptly describes my situation. How dare I shield myself from this truth as prevalent as it was in its first two decades, that which had such impact on my community! How dare I believe that it could not affect my circle! That I was buffered; AIDS reduced down, chalked up, to a headline, a broadcast, something that people who were not like me suffered, something that people who were careless or uninformed suffered. Today I would like to think that if I had known about Lawrence, Laurence and Bernard, I would have come running in the pouring rain to stand beside them in their final hours. I did not even think to check on them after graduation, to inquire after them, my blood brothers, during a crisis that I knew was striking down lives indiscriminately.

This brings me to the prevalent arrogance and ignorance that exists at a national level, where the number of deaths and infections are still rising, and affecting demographics worldwide. Where apprehensions about an open, honest dialogue on sex and sexuality still prevents us from saving lives. Where despite the fact that there is so much money spent on preventative measures for other health issues, not enough is designated to this disease or reaches the people truly in need: the financially disadvantaged, the uninsured and under-insured, the young, the uneducated.

What have you learned from your life? What will you take with you when you die?

I remember my friend Ted Kirk, whom I helped to take care of up until his dying day. I remember his wispy blonde hair, his smiling eyes and broad laugh. I remember feeding him his dinner when he could no longer feed himself. I remember helping him bathe and use the bathroom and getting him in and out of bed. I remember sitting with him for long stretches in the evenings as we watched *Law & Order*, one of his favorite television shows. I remember when he had to be moved to a hospice, and the people there who were so pleasant and worked so tirelessly. I remember him marrying his boyfriend from a wheelchair, his dementia, and the times when I thought he would not make it through another night; then finally his quiet death, like a light summer breeze that enters a room and just as effortlessly exits.

When I die I am determined to leave behind my ignorance, for Earth is the only place where it belongs. I shall leave behind my regrets as well, becoming weightless and free. What is past has passed. I will take with me only my memories of loves, lovers and friends; of sunny, golden days long gone. And of the work I have done here on Earth and the people I have met. I will also take with me the days of Lawrence and Laurence and Bernard. I will cherish our fun together as children in the face of life's harsh realities, our laughter, our finite number of memories. And of the lessons they taught me, which I will forever hold dear to my heart.

LUCKY THIRTEEN

THERE I STOOD, as if on a precipice, at that age all young adults eventually come to inhabit. The age of awkwardness, the age between here and there, of resentfulness and anger; of alternating waves of unexplainable apprehension and moodiness. Young adults hit this stage like a brick wall. Suddenly, it's a wake up call to impending adulthood where they are no longer kids but still feel childlike in their hearts and minds. Where they are no longer treated with the delicacy of a child, as they were only a few years prior. Almost as if overnight their black and white reasoning has landed them in a world that seems unfairly colorized. For any young adult, it is both an exasperating and deeply emotional evolution. Sins are not so easily forgiven and rules become much more sternly enforced. To further complicate matters, it is a time of rebirth. The body is changing, feelings are developing, and for the first time perhaps the young person obtains the first glimpses of the power they will possess as adults.

I arrived at this milestone amid the turmoil of my home life. The relationship with my mother was at its worst. There was nothing I could do or say that was right, and I was feeling increasing alienation from my family, paired with a depression only young adults can know. I felt as if no one understood, or cared to understand, anything I thought or said. That this abusive relationship with my mother was not only killing my spirit but would only grow worse and more damaging over time. This developed into a dark period for me where I withdrew from everyone, and in this course–whether by fate, luck or happenstance–I became aware of my undiscovered self.

I was at that time in my life a very sensitive soul. I thought a lot, daydreamed plenty, felt deeply. This was also when I purchased my first grown-up novel. Cliche as it may sound, it was as if bells went off inside me, a light bulb flashed above my head, and suddenly all that sensitivity had a channel and I developed a prophetic vision, a greater understanding of the route my life would take. It was the start of summer in my thirteenth year that I bought Stephen King's *The Shining*, a novel about a family who runs a grand Denver hotel with a rich and notorious past, only to have the reader wonder if it is the malicious ghosts of the hotel or the protagonist's bout with alcoholism that truly haunts this family nearly to death. I purchased the book from a pharmacy, back when pharmacies were family-owned and carried paperback novels. Before you scoff, I consider that work–one of my favorites by King–to be one of the best finds of my life. It was a milestone that would mark the beginning of my love affair with reading. You see, I finished the more than three hundred page book in about a week and went out to buy another, *Christine*, King's story of an awkward and unpopular teen who buys his first car, only to find that the automobile is not only haunted but murderous and nearly unstoppable. I went on from there to read *Carrie*, *Salem's Lot*, *The Dead Zone*, *Cujo*, and *Firestarter*.

By July, I figured I would explore something more ambitious. I was drawn to John Jakes, the historical novelist who published *North and South*, *Love and War*, and *Heaven and Hell*, three books that dealt with the Civil War from the point of view of two men, and their families, friends who eventually realized their sympathies fell on opposite sides of the conflict. I read all three by the end of August and when school started I was hungry for more. I was fortunate to have an English teacher who seemed hell-bent on having her students read novels among their other assignments. I started with *Things Fall Apart* by Chinua Achebe, and moved on to Charles Dickens's *Great Expectations*, *Nicholas Nickelby*, and *Oliver Twist*.

There was also the predictable high school reads: Melville's *Barteleby*, Tolkien's *The Hobbit*, C.S. Lewis' *The Lion, the Witch, and the Wardrobe*, Hemingway's *The Old Man and The Sea* and *Of Mice and Men*, and Lee's *To Kill a Mockingbird*. By the end of the school year, we had gotten around to Shelly's *Frankenstein*, H.G. Wells' *The Island of Dr. Moreau*, Dumas' *The Count of Monte Cristo*, Thomas Hardy's *The Mayor of Casterbridge*, and Golding's *Lord of the Flies*. I had never read so much so quickly. And yet, by the time summer came around again, I was devoted to spending a summer reading on my own, investigating titles I'd seen in a used bookstore not far from where I lived. To me bookstores are like bakeries, where everything looks good and one is never enough.

That was the summer I discovered an author, and a title, that would forever change my life: James Baldwin. We were required to read in class one of his titles called *Go Tell It on the Mountain*, a novel told from various points of view, examining the impact of the church in the lives of African-Americans. While I found the work terribly dense, on par with Toni Morrison, I recall the language made a huge impression on me. It was exquisitely written with colorful passages and entrancing, believable characters, and it explored its topic as thoroughly as any book I'd read up to that time. Another of his works, *Giovanni's Room*, caught my eye that summer; it was a revelation. Baldwin's second published novel was about the struggles of a male protagonist as he grapples with sex, sexuality and alienation in both the United States and Europe. Although I was just 14, the themes spoke to the very heart of my identity and it was the first time I began to see books as an avenue to understanding one's self as opposed to just entertainment.

The next milestone came at the start of the following school year when Arlene Bernstein became my new English teacher. She was rumored to be tough and believed in hard work and pushing her students to their fullest capabilities. Oddly enough, she became the best instructor I would ever have. Outside of grammar and vocabulary, she had a deep love of literature. We started the year by reading plays. Among other playwrights: the works of Shakespeare, Eugene O'Neil, and Tennessee Williams. Sophocles's tragedies *Oedipus Tyrannus*, *Oedipus at Colonus*, and *Antigone*. Then we moved on to poetry, examining *Ode to a Grecian Urn* and progressing through *Dover Beach* and *For A Lady I Know*. We burned through works by Nikki Giovanni, Langston Hughes, Walt Whitman, Maya Angelou, T.S. Elliot, Robert Frost, and William Carlos Williams. We read Greek mythology, *Beowulf* and John Donne's *Meditation 17*. The line "No man is an island entire of himself" still serves as a reminder to me when I feel that I am guarding myself too much from others and the sometimes harsh and negative world around me. We read Harriet Beecher Stowe, Percy Bysshe Shelley, E.M. Forster, and F. Scott Fitzgerald. By the time the school year was over, Mrs. Bernstein had mercy on her students: the last two months were spent studying the art of the short story, including *The Lottery* by Shirley Jackson, *Young Goodman Brown* by Nathaniel Hawthorne, *An Occurrence at Owl Creek Bridge* by Ambrose Bierce, *The Tell-Tale Heart* by Edgar Allen Poe, *The*

Legend of Sleepy Hollow by Washington Irving, and *The Monkey's Paw* by W.W. Jacobs.

What intrigued me about this class was that unlike the previous year, where I'd spent a great deal of time devouring books, Mrs. Bernstein introduced us to the practice of understanding a work and all its intents and purposes. Not only were we to read the literature, but we were to be prepared to adequately explain and discuss the symbolism in *Young Goodman Brown*, the social relevance of Countee Cullen's *For A Lady I Know*, the overarching themes in Miller's *Death of a Salesman*, and the impact of Randall Jarrell's *The Death of the Ball Turret Gunner*. For us boys, reading *The Color Purple* was an exercise in removing ourselves from our place of comfort to walk in someone else's shoes (in this instance, that of the opposite sex), while dissecting the tragic *Oedipus* forced the class to objectively confront complex issues.

But Arlene Bernstein taught me more than the beginning lessons of critical thinking. She also provided me a home away from home, a means of escape, a purpose. She taught me how to seek and root out truth and meaning to the events in my life, to understand my heart and motivations as a budding adult, to understand symbolism in everyday life, and to use writers and their protagonists as inspiration. But most importantly, she taught me to think outside myself and to see a world that was larger and greater, and to find resource, pleasure and comfort in

50

something as simple as reading. Yes, I remain a fan of Stephen King, and have read a good deal of Sidney Sheldon, Agatha Christie, Amy Tan, George Pelecanos, J.K. Rowling, Michael Crichton, John Irving and Dominick Dunne among many others. But because of Arlene Bernstein I have dared to explore on my own such writers as Virginia Woolf, Lillian Hellman, Frederick Douglas, Richard Wright, Toni Morrison, August Wilson, Alice Walker, Gabriel Garcia Marquez, Jhumpa Lahiri, Gore Vidal, Oscar Wilde, Edward Albee, Jane Smiley, Pablo Neruda, and Tony Kushner.

I have read nearly every work published by James Baldwin and Edith Wharton, respectively my favorite writers. Baldwin's *Another Country* is my favorite novel with its bold, violent language, its anti-heroic characters in a constant state of struggle and turmoil, its fearless and complex examination of race relations, sex, sexuality, and the seemingly inexplicable relationships between men and women, and men and men. It surprises and moves me every time I read it. Who would predict its down-on-his-luck protagonist Rufus Scott would commit suicide eighty pages into the novel, leaving in his wake a group of friends to stir within the cauldron of their own conflicting emotions and desires.

Edith Wharton, on the other hand, produced one of my favorite novels *The Age of Innocence*. She also wrote *Summer*, *Roman Fever, Ethan Frome*, and *Old New York*. But it is *The Age of*

Innocence that captures and examines the traps of high society, and as a by-product, "celebrity," like no other work. Wharton's well-to-do characters, who on the surface should be happy to have everything at their disposal are instead miserable in their repetitive lives: day after day the rotating dinners, operas, balls, house calls, and arranged marriages, the trap of "civilized" living to which they all aspire is also a prison. There is no variety here in their daily lives, alternately providing comfort and stagnation. When the Countess Olenska arrives from Europe fresh out of a failed marriage, not only is she stunningly beautiful and sensuous, she is bohemian—the antithesis of her new environment. It becomes plain that she has struck the interest of her cousin's fiancé Newland Archer, and this places a target on her back as well as his. They inspire gossip and become a source of entertainment to society's most powerful citizens, and then like a cat bored with its captive mouse, they destroy their union, bringing about a very tragic and miserable conclusion for Archer. Mirrored against modern-day celebrity, Wharton's work seems prophetic regarding the human desire for prestige and wealth and the suffering that often comes with them. To this day, I am not quite certain a man could have written this novel with the sharp, balanced description of celebrity and yearning.

Baldwin and Wharton made such a profound impression on me that I read everything about their own lives. How Baldwin was a novice writer who believed neither he nor his writing would be understood or appreciated. He was, after all, a homosexual Negro in 1940s America, writing with unapologetic and unerring intellectual aim about such inflammatory topics as race relations between Blacks and Whites. Baldwin appealed to writer Richard Wright, who wrote *Black Boy* and *The Outsider*, to become his mentor. Wright was an expatriate of the United States living in France. I read about how their relationship flourished and imploded when Baldwin wrote *Everybody's Protest Novel*, an essay taking to task the actions and motivations of Wright's protagonist Bigger Thomas from *Native Son*. The relationship between Baldwin and Wright was irreparable because of this. I learned how Baldwin's support of Martin Luther King, Jr.'s fight for Negro equality was a tricky exercise because of his homosexuality.

Wharton, meanwhile, began writing very young in life. She was so hungry with literary ambitions that she used the brown parcel paper on packages delivered to her parents' home to write on when no other paper was available. Wharton's father who grew up with and inherited substantial wealth, lacked personal ambition—and her mother was, if not outright hostile toward her, cold with indifference. Wharton's work often dealt with the elements of the environment into which she was born in 1862, as a resident of Old New York with the ability to view firsthand the restraints of high society. While she wrote on these very subjects with precision in such novels as *The House of Mirth*, she herself moved about her life not as a woman of her time. She married and divorced at an early age, was a renowned author long before the Jazz Age, emerged herself in World War I by taking up causes of the Allied forces and becoming the head of the American Hostels for Refugees, and taking up permanent residence in France in 1913.

Even though my reading has moved into other areas (I am a sucker for well-penned books on business, biographies and topical non-fiction), I now also seek out works by foreign and first-time authors who deserve as much recognition as they can get as they embark on their careers. Works of excellence by LGBT authors also fall into this category, as well as editors and authors who produce anthologies or collections of short stories. Still, I like to keep one foot in the past by reading from my personal library Grace Metalious's *Peyton Place* or Kahlil Gibran's *The Prophet* or essays by Essex Hemphill.

It is with a heavy heart then that I must confess that I hear far too many people admit to me these days that they are just not readers. When I think of all the wonderful works that have been produced–that are still being produced–I find it to be akin to an act of violence against writers everywhere, or at the very least it shows a lack of imagination, or an intellectual laziness. I sometimes wonder what type of person I'd be if I'd not read Paul Monette's remarkable *Becoming a Man* or Katherine Graham's *Personal History* or Lawrence Otis Graham's *Our Kind of People*. Have movies, video games, television, wireless devices, and countless hours spent online stupefied the modern-day brain to such an extent that we fail to recognize the joys of employing the imagination through reading? Are we failing as a race by not passing down from generation to generation the important legacy of reading: of the enlightenment to be gained, and the people, lands, worlds, and times to be discovered?

Part of me believes that much of today's generation does not read, because they suffer from a lack of a well-executed introduction to reading and to the classics. For me it started out with horror because it was entertaining, but the real credit goes to my two English instructors who chose works they knew students would find stimulating. In countless conversations with friends, many admit they have not read even half of the books I have mentioned in this essay, and I can only say to them with amazement: What did you do in high school and at university? What did you do with your summers? And given that times have changed, I wonder what books young people read today. While there has been a deserved excitement over the J.K. Rowling *Harry Potter* series that have spurred in young people a new desire to read, there remain centuries of work that I fear are gathering dust on library shelves, unexplored. What is more disheartening is that women read more than men, older individuals read more than younger ones, books are perhaps read less than magazines, which are perhaps read more than newspapers nowadays; and the average article has cut its word limit, because the attention span of the reader has diminished over the years.

There are two images that I remember from my youth that spook me to this day. One is of the original motion picture adaptation of H.G. Wells's *The Time Machine*, when the Rod Taylor character H. George Wells discovers the timid and complacent Eloi people of the future don't know how to read and he travels back to his own time to pick up three books to take back with him to the future in order to teach them and rebuild civilization. The viewer is left to wonder what three books he took and what three books they would take. The other is of the famous Rod Serling *Twilight Zone* episode *Time Enough to Last*, when Burgess Meredith's character Henry Bemis, a nerdy henpecked bookworm, is the only person left alive after an atomic explosion and he can read as much as he likes without interruption. That is until he drops his spectacles, breaking both lenses beyond repair and is left crying about the unfairness of his predicament.

Reading was my savior, a sort of surrogate parent. I turned to books for information on subjects neither of my parents would discuss with me. I am thankful for this gift that puts me in touch with myself and the world around me. I am all too aware that there are people still in this world who are illiterate and that there was once a time in the United States' history when it was illegal and punishable for Black slaves to be found reading, even the

Bible. Any author worth his salt will tell you writing is not easy. It is difficult, time consuming, and often unrewarding. But despite themselves they are compelled to do what some would label as God's work: in illuminating, enriching and enlightening. So when you see a young person just sitting around doing nothing, be sure to hand them a book. At first something entertaining, like a fun mystery, something spooky, or an adventure novel to whet their appetite. Discuss with them the book's themes. And soon, like a bike, they'll be riding on their own; the world ahead of them like a stretch of beautiful road filled with wonder and mystery. Thom and Huck would be proud.

DOVE

AND THERE CAME a day quite unlike any other. It was the day when I came to know a girl who would change my life forever, in ways I am sure she could not comprehend at the time, nor for which she would ever have volunteered had she known the hard, cold and conflicted truth that was me. I hurt her in ways no man should ever hurt a woman. I lied to her, causing her more grief and pain than she deserved in ten lifetimes. Should she come to read this—while it is certain she will never forgive me—I want her to know that I will always love her and her good heart. That I will always be ashamed of the misery I brought to her life, and for causing bitterness I am confident remains harbored within her to this very day.

THIS WAS NOT kismet. Our meeting was arranged and not something either of us set out to initiate. I had noticed her around school from the start of the season, although we did not share any of the same classes. Her name was Yolanda Dove and she was a tall, light-skinned African-American sophomore with very smooth skin and short, curled hair. We had a mutual friend named Kala Cunningham, who was in a good number of my classes. Kala was a fun and funny girl who chewed gum loudly and ran with the sports crowd. I am not sure why she thought Yolanda and I would make a great couple, but she used her matchmaking skills to set us up–an event that would take my life in a direction I could never have foreseen; although I knew in my heart that it would have a lasting effect.

I remember when I was introduced to Yolanda. It was during homeroom period, and this particular morning was fairly forgettable beyond the fact that it was unusually bright and sunny. Kala had asked Yolanda to stop by so they could walk and gossip on their way to their next class, but once in my company Kala abandoned Yolanda, leaving the two of us to deduce—as we stood alone in a suddenly empty room–that we had been set up. I don't remember what Yolanda was wearing, but I do remember her face: the arched black eyebrows, the light, smooth, evenly-toned skin of her face, her pouty lips shiny with gloss. My heart was rhythmic in my ears and I became aware that the crotch of my pants grew uncomfortably taut with each passing second. I hid it sheepishly behind my schoolbag.

Our initial conversation volleyed back and forth.

"How are you?"

"Fine."

"Your name is Hassan, right?"

"Yeah; it means handsome or beautiful, or to make handsome or beautiful."

"You Muslim?"

"No, Catholic."

"That Kala."

"I know.

"I'll get her later."

"She's a riot."

"What should we do?"

"I don't know."

"You want to play along?"

"That would be fun."

I didn't know then why we felt it necessary to pretend to make a connection, but in hindsight it's quite clear. Our private life was so complicated that we wanted to it keep secret from each other for as long as possible. And while there was a definite attraction between us, I believe we rushed into a union to bring some form of normalcy to our lives, some rosy color: the promise of romance, the joy of young love. We joined forces to right the wrongs of our lives, and as many young people believe: to take charge of our destiny in hopes of bypassing our parents' mistakes. We would be the young lovers against the world, doing it right, leaving the mess that was our home lives behind. The school would become our Utopia, where we could control the storyline.

On the surface, the union worked in many ways. You could say that we were an outcast among our own sex. I was the smart, well-dressed kid who lived downtown but who stood apart from the jocks, the nerds, the jokers, the hell-raisers; I related to all of them and none of them simultaneously. She was a bit of a tomboy from the gruff north side of Philadelphia, and while she was not what I would label as model pretty, she was certainly attractive enough to catch the eye of every guy in school. And she was friends with enough of them to make more than a few of the popular girls jealous.

Our pairing made for fodder: it was very clear we were polar opposites. I was short, she was tall; I was labeled a preppie, she was rather casual; we traveled in two different directions on our way home: she uptown, me down. But what was not so apparent to everyone was our need to comfort each other. For as no-nonsense as Yolanda could be at times, her voice was almost always soft and accommodating. When she spoke, I could feel the ice melt from my heart. Her voice was so warm and appealing that when I close my eyes I can still hear it; I can still sleep to it. On the other hand, I was an emotionally scarred animal, and what I offered to her was passion. I was her cheerleader to get out in the world and never give in, to never back down, to never be afraid to dream or be herself. The war at home with my mother was building into a daily and furious crescendo, from which I needed solace. In Yolanda's house, there was her mother Alice and brother Donald. Alice raised

61

Yolanda and Donald, for the most part, alone. And while Yolanda loved her mother a great deal, the family lived on a strict budget that seemed to serve as a constant reminder of the hardships of Yolanda's early years. It was clear she needed sunshine and laughter.

In the beginning, we were happy. Our manufactured relationship allowed us to become friends first. We talked a great deal: in between classes, at lunch, in the library, after school, during extracurricular activities. We adopted each other's friends: Kala, April Staton, Laurence Gray, Bernard Little, Curtis Ghee, Ronald Mitchell, Debbie Williams, Ian Smart, Noble Ramsey. Faced with the alternative that was my home life, I looked forward to going to school; it was like a television show of sorts, where we were the center of this universe of outrageous characters. It was Yolanda who got me involved in the Drama and Debate clubs. It was Yolanda's love for Michael Jackson that convinced me to listen to the music of Prince and The Culture Club and Madonna. It was she who thought we should adopt Cyndi Lauper's *Time After Time* as Our Song. Yes, things progressed very well at the start, but that was only until it was time to reveal our feelings, to stop playing poker and to show our hands. And that was only half of the problem.

Before anything else could be confronted, there were our families. It was clear that we had different upbringings. At times it was evident in the conversations we'd share, in the way we handled conflict or a difference of opinion. She was a girl who was very tough on the outside, her mother's nickname for her was Tuffy. But Yolanda was also very feminine and would tear up at the drop of the hat, sometimes at songs or something she saw. I found this to be mysterious, and now looking back: charming. I had learned over the years to cement my emotions and drown them. At home my feelings carried no weight, and I became so disconnected from them that I forgot how to be sympathetic or empathetic. There were many times I appeared flat out insensitive and aloof. And as if by morning sunlight that seeps through blinds or cascades over the horizon, Yolanda and I began to see each other through glasses tainted by our pasts.

This caused turbulence in our pretend relationship. Because I was willfully blind to the fact that she had developed strong feelings for me, I was confused as to why she constantly felt the need to discuss every conflict that developed between us. I was unaccustomed to handling relationships in that manner, and I came out of each of our spats appearing cold and unfeeling. Unaware of how to quell these situations I broke off the relationship. For me, it was easier this way; safer than having to explain my home life and the way I was raised.

We eventually found our way back to each other, as we often did whenever I left her—which I did a great deal during our relationship. Nearly every time a situation brought us closer to a certain truth about me, one that I was ill-quipped to handle, I would shut myself in a fortress of solitude. I would later have a fraternity brother who would scream at me that whenever something went wrong with me, I retreated into this fortress where no one is permitted access. The first time this happened it was because Yolanda wanted to meet my family and was very angry when I would not invite her to my home or give her my phone number. What she did not know was that I had a mother who disapproved of nearly everything I did, and introducing her into that cyclone of negativity would subject the both of us to an excruciating embarrassment that I wished to avoid at all costs.

Yolanda was crushed when I rebuffed her and after much needling from her friends, I eventually gave in. As it turned out, my mother did indeed dislike her immensely. She even told me years after Yolanda and I had been dating: *Hassan, you cannot marry this girl. You must not marry beneath you.* My mother was frosty toward her from day one; she never approved of her. And I was never sure if it was Yolanda and her background that upset my mother or the fact that she simply did not want to give me any positive affirmation. Similarly, Yolanda's mother Alice was distrustful of me. At our initial meeting her eyes bore into me. From this gaze I gleaned that she had perhaps had difficulty with men and here I was knocking on her daughter's door, a new generation of prospective heartache.

I would not say that Yolanda and I escaped this vortex entirely; we merely sidestepped it. She was never invited to my home and I limited her phone calls. I did likewise on visits and contacting her. It remained difficult on us as a couple, but I also believe it was what spurred us to make this union official. We clung to each other like a life raft, making the most out of every special occasion: birthdays, holidays, Valentine's Day. I remember the first gift I ever bought her: a gold heart locket on a chain. On one Valentine's Day she gave me a decorative mug printed with a poem about love. Through the ups and downs of our relationship, the break-ups and the make-ups, we returned to each other and assumed the stance: as the only other person on the face of the earth to whom we had opened our hearts. Except that wasn't completely true.

By the time we entered college, we had settled into our roles as boyfriend and girlfriend to the extent that we entered into a universal tug of war (known otherwise as the battle of the sexes). But there was something else that had not been confronted and that perhaps added to the tension: intimacy. Yes, there had been kissing and hugging and petting, but we hadn't had sex. There were two reasons for this. No one, specifically my mother, had discussed sex with me, except to tell me that it took only one sexual encounter to result in pregnancy. I am assuming now that she was speaking from experience, as my birth was not planned (and even at my young age I was firm in the belief that I did not wish to repeat my immediate family's cycle of bad parenting).

While that caused more than its fair share of trepidation, I was still a young man with a growing curiosity and a healthy arsenal of raging hormones. And therein lies the problem.

While I was in love with Yolanda and had plans on building a life with her, I was keenly aware, as I had been since a very early age, that I was attracted to both sexes. To this day I find women to be beautiful, if frustrating, creatures. A large part of their actions remain difficult for me to decipher (a claim I am certain they could just as easily make about men), but all the same I find them lovely. There is something sexy and arousing about the softness of their hair, the delicacy of their faces, or how our hands can slip down the sides of a woman's body, starting wide and outlining the orbs of her breasts, dipping in, and shifting out along her hourglass figure, the perfume on her neck bringing to mind the color powder blue. And as any person who really loves women can tell you: while good sex can be something akin to storming a castle, the constant mystery that is her heart is the real treasure. Winning a woman's heart is a challenging expedition that can only be done by truly understanding it. On the other hand with men the attraction for me has always been more organic. Whether it is physical or figurative, it is a man's strength that I am attracted to, that gets my heart racing. He too is a domain to be investigated and conquered; his intellect to be challenged, his personality to be decoded, the true nature of his power (be it physical or otherwise) to be soused out and compared to mine, with nothing less than all the passion he possesses. And while there are certain physical characteristics that attract me more than others, I have never, ever been attracted to a weak man. It is a man's confidence that I find sexually enticing, his hearty laugh, his ambition, his intellectual prowess, and his comfort in his own skin. But what attracts me most is how men can openly and graphically talk to each other (be they merely friends or more), and at times while being in the company of one another: speaking without speaking.

This inner conflict proved confusing to me in my early years. I could not think clearly on this issue, and times were not as they are now, with a seemingly exponential evolution forward that includes more acceptance and understanding and positive representation–at least in certain sections of the world. I had my family to think about, my reputation, my career, and my relationship with Yolanda. So I lied to her more than once, making her believe that I was busy or preoccupied with work or school, that she was crowding me, and I kept her at arms length as long as I could until I could make a decision about what it was I exactly wanted, trying desperately not to make a permanent mistake or a wrong move. Trying desperately not to hurt her or me or anyone. All this while I was at university, while I was working, while I was dealing with the soap opera that was my mother, was more than I could handle and so I chose the easy path out, the safest one. I asked Yolanda if she would marry me

67

and she said she would. I had never been with another man during my time with her and I had only ever kissed one other girl: a previous girlfriend when I was thirteen. I figured that what I didn't know about men wouldn't hurt me. I would immerse myself in our marriage and I would drown out every curiosity that burned within my desire. Needless to say, that didn't work out so well and my relationship with Yolanda was never the same after I made the admission to her years later that I was bisexual.

CALL ME IGNORANT, stupid, and naive if you must, but I should have seen the writing on the wall. I should have known that I could not change who I am. I lost my virginity to Yolanda on my twenty-first birthday, and I think she and I could both say that while the evening started out lovely with a bubble bath and dinner, I was not exactly a whiz kid in bed. I had no clue what to do. Pornography was not so mainstream back then (later serving as a visual learning tool for all young rabbits working their way out of the hutch), so I relied on stories I'd heard from other guys, taking instruction from them. The result was disastrous. Certain things I got right; many things I got wrong. Intimacy became spotty sooner rather than later, and I was frustrated with myself and frustrated with the relationship, because while she loved me I knew I was not making her happy.

She had cried so many times during our relationship, and she cried doubly so when I finally ended it after seven years. It was in October I remember, near Halloween. I had left her so many times that it became a ritual she expected every couple of years. She was burned and burned out. Bitter. Desperate for a happiness that would never come her way from me. It embarrassed and hurt me to end things, but I saw clearly that it hurt her more deeply that I wrung her out as I did. I had used up every benefit of the doubt, all grace periods, and too many acts of forgiveness. To this day my grandmother still asks after her, and it hurts me because I know Yolanda hates me.

Years later we ran into each other. I had moved on with many girlfriends after her, and none of them seemed to fit quite right. Yolanda was a hard act to follow. But I had also moved on with a good number of male partners, and the tug of war between the two sexes remained in my life. When she returned, this issue had still not been resolved. Bisexuals are often seen as people who cannot make up their mind one way or the other, and I did nothing to dispel that fallacy. While it did not seem to matter to men that I had been with women, it mattered a great deal to women that I had been with men. This scorched me, because once again it did not seem as if I could please everyone or anyone. The only bright spot in all of this was that during Yolanda's time away I came out to my family, relieving myself of doing something I absolutely detest: lying. By the time I had revealed to her this whole truth, we had just started spending time together, getting back into our old routine. I now realize that she wanted me back. After I told her she stopped talking to me, she stopped returning my phone calls, and then she disappeared from my life.

I have seen her once since then. We bumped into each other one day. She was bitter, nasty, and ruthlessly rude; she figured I deserved it. Sadly, I agree. Out of all of this I have learned that one must be truthful no matter how difficult it may be. My omission of the truth cost Yolanda seven years of her life and created in her a mistrust of men I am sure she still has to this day. There have been many stories of late about guys on the down low: men who have sex with men while in relationships with women. I believe there is nothing so hurtful to a woman as a lie of the heart, particularly an infidelity, and especially one with which she cannot compete. I hurt Yolanda with my stalling and indecision, and there are many men out there who are doing the same. I cannot provide a blanket condemnation of their actions, for every indecision and lie has its reason, but men must be men or else we are not fit to call ourselves men at all. This means being considerate, taking into account the consequences of our actions, and realizing that the repercussion of our choices can impact and derail another person's life for many, many years. This is a call to consciousness and consideration and responsibility. I know a woman whose name is Yolanda Dove and because I was not honest and open I have ruined any chance of a friendship we could have had. She was and remains the only woman to ever place herself so deeply in my heart.

I CANNOT SAY that my dating life has improved very much at all. I've had some hits. I've had some definite misses. Times have changed. Dating is different, complicated, tricky. I can say one thing with pride: I am different. I am truthful. Some find it a relief; others find it to be too much information. Regardless, one day I'd like to find a soulmate and be married. I'd like some children, biological or adopted. I'm not sure that's likely to happen, but it won't be for a lack of trying or for a lack of being honest and frank about who and what I am and what I want. It is only a shame that sometimes learning and evolution come at the expense of others. For that, I am sorry, Yolanda. Please accept my heartfelt apology. I never, ever meant to hurt you.

CLOSER

MY FATHER DIED the evening of Monday, November 6, 2000.

I still remember every detail of his death and funeral. I remember clearly the urgent calls from my sister and the mad rush to the hospital where I was too late to say good-bye. The days following stretched out like endless miles of tumultuous ocean ending at his funeral. Days that I could not eat or sleep—days I slept too much. Days that I was incoherent, moody, and more than anything, lost. Days that I cried so long and so hard that it felt like I was attempting to weep away every ounce of pain I felt with his passing.

I am my father's eldest son, the first of his four children. To say that my dad and I shared a turbulent relationship would be a gross understatement. As a young man, I blamed him for almost everything wrong in my life: my broken family, his remarrying and his second family, his alcoholism, even his parenting skills. He on the other hand found it nearly impossible to accept the truth regarding my sexuality. When reflecting on that period, I can honestly say that I was angry because circumstances seemed to conspire that we could not be simpatico. His divorce from my mother and their constant battles truly changed the course of our lives. My father seemed regretful that all that lay between us–our past, our issues–would prevent us from ever becoming close.

Time eventually changed that situation, and years later, after he became seriously ill, we reconciled and vowed to become the father and son we should have been. But before that dream could be fully realized, he died. Five years after we had made our reaffirming pact, I found myself within a well of pain and regret that I never knew could extend so deeply. His sudden passing from my life took my breath away, and instantly and sharply, I mourned his loss. I could not help but remember our angry words and animosity. What we had was a type of emotional pain that only fathers and sons can inflict on each other.

It's funny how some lessons in life come quickly and while others take a lifetime. On the day of my father's funeral, I had to visit the old neighborhood. The services were being held there, at the church where my parents were married. Across the street stood my grandmother's house, though she had passed away many years ago. Looking at it I was suddenly reminded of my past there, of a simpler time, before things got complicated between my father and me. I remembered summer days that seemed endless, slow warm nights that seemed to drag on forever and skies filled with countless stars. My brother and I racing wildly up and down the street with the neighborhood kids until all hours. Baseball games on my first transistor radio. Piles of comic books. Building a dog house. A frenetic dash for the ice cream truck. Fried fish on Fridays and elaborate Sunday dinners that hardly anyone seems to have any longer. The stillness and quiet of the large house on a lazy Saturday afternoon. The sun and its dancing, sparkling lights pouring in through the skylight from the third floor. The sanctuary of the kitchen, clean and serene, as Sinatra or Nat King Cole played on the radio.

When I stood to speak about my father during the funeral, a powerful feeling came over me. As if I was to glean something from this very instant, of this particular week when I mentally rummaged through a photo box of memories in between choosing the day of our final goodbye, the suit my father would wear eternally, and the casket he would call home. As if this were an *Aha!* moment in which I was to discover a revelation. And it was. Looking out over the attendees, I was amazed at the size of the audience. The church was filled! So many people: friends, relatives, boyhood pals, colleagues, people I hardly knew and some I did not know at all. At that moment, all at once, it came together. My tempestuous life with my father, the carefree sunny days of my early youth, the funeral day stark in its reality, all together made sense. Not only had I inherited my

74

father's role as head of his family (both a burden and an honor), I was to cherish this life as the two of us had failed to do. I was to cherish it and value it at every second.

It struck me as I composed the eulogy that these people were all part of my father's life, his history. They too had a past with my father filled with sunny days and cherished memories, as I had with my brother when I was younger. Because of our estrangement, I had missed out on this part of my father's life, on whom he truly was as a person independent of fatherhood. I felt suddenly embarrassed and ashamed at the cliché: I had allowed my father to die without fully knowing him. I had failed in paying him the highest tribute a son could pay a father: understanding him, as we all yearn to be understood. My anger and bitter words had played a part in preventing us from becoming closer. And I now thought if I had just given in, given up, compromised more, if I had just *tried harder*. Now my father was gone. It was a feeling so indescribably painful and frightening, that my own mortality overwhelmed me. I could die without ever being truly known or understood by those closest to me. I was an accident, an unplanned pregnancy that resulted in my parents getting married (a secret recently disclosed to me by my father's mother). Whether true or not, I have always believed that without my conception he would never have engaged in such a disastrous marriage to my mother, and his alcoholism–precipitated out of this union to a woman he loved but who may never have truly loved or understood him–might

75

have been avoided entirely. It has always been my secret belief that my father's immediate family failed him. My mother, yes; but as his eldest child, certainly I had too. It was my job to understand him; that was my duty.

When the funeral was over, all my father's friends came to me to shake my hand, to give me a hug, and to tell me how wonderful my dad was. How he was such a loyal friend, supportive, funny, outrageous. Tales they knew that I didn't. Tales I was ashamed I didn't know. They told me he loved his family and was proud of his children, especially me. I was taken aback at this, because he never told me as much; perhaps only because I never really gave him the opportunity.

Strangely in his death my dad is closer to me now. I feel him all around, I see him in my dreams, in faces on the street. He counsels me in spirit, advising me against his mistakes, urging me to learn from his accomplishments: make friends, be good to people, let your light shine, work hard, love your family. I talk to him in prayers and meditation, share with him, exposing to him my deepest fears of isolation, of failure, of living regretfully. As a result, it is as if he has become more powerful in death than he ever was in my life. And there is not a time when I do not feel him around me, or in me. Although I cannot change the past, I now have with him the relationship I have always wanted.

Even now, when I look at my sister's son, so handsome and active, I see my father in him. I see myself in him. I see at once, in his wondrous, stubborn eyes, the past and future of my family. I am confident that things will be different between the two of us. We will be better, closer. He doesn't understand why I stare at him as he plays endlessly with his toys, why I tell him so often that I love him. Or why there are tears in my eyes when I hug him so very tightly before he goes home. But he will one day, of that I am sure. Life is funny like that: unyielding in its lessons.

PART TWO

FIRST PERSON SINGULAR

THE ONE THAT GOT AWAY

ONE OF THE things I despise most in this world is the use of religion to assume an advantaged position. There are far too many instances of this practice throughout the history of man to enumerate here and now. A massive list could be composed of this infraction just since the start of the 20th century, let alone any period prior. In fact, civilizations have been constructed upon this Machiavellian moral one-upmanship. Where we have prided ourselves in recent years as an advanced people educated with lessons learned from history and diversity to yield a more tolerant and empathetic society, it would strangely appear as if we have also redefined the statement one step forward, two steps back.

As I sit penning this essay, there brews in New York City a controversy involving the erection of a community center for Muslims to be built two city streets away from the site of the tragic episode that occurred at the World Trade Center in lower Manhattan on the morning of September 11, 2001. At the height of this debate between those who would seemingly condemn every living Muslim's right to have a community center near this hallowed ground and those who comprehend a danger in doing so (labeling it bigotry), stands pastor Terry Jones. Up until the day of the ninth anniversary of 9/11 he threatened to hold an event at his Florida church where copies of the Islamic holy book, the Quran, would be burned as an act of protest against the location of the mosque. No good could come from this, nor any sense of clarity on the underlying matter, and yet Jones embraced this blasphemous act as deserved retribution. Reckless as this was, it only served as kindling for an already volatile situation and dangerous worldwide for American military personnel stationed in countries with large populations of already-agitated Muslims.

This behavior is not unprecedented, most notably in the actions of the controversial Reverend Fred Phelps, who, in 2006, led a protest at the military funeral of Lance Corporal Matthew Snyder. Snyder, at the young age of twenty, gave his life fighting in the United States war in Iraq. In return, Phelps led the congregation from Westboro Baptist Church in Topeka, Kansas to picket his funeral, having claimed that American soldiers were evil in that they defending a country where homosexuality was tolerated. Snyder's family and friends who had come to respectfully mourn their loss found this to be appalling.

In a much more domestic matter, in 2008 a Saudi man killed his daughter for converting to Christianity. The man, a member of Promotion of Virtue and Prevention of Vice, cut her tongue and burned her to death following heated debates over religion. Contrary to the actions of these and other dubious religious leaders—in and of themselves extremists—my faith in religion remains unwavering. In my mind these acts are the work of man, not God nor his true disciples and certainly not in the interest to further the principles of compassion and fellowship. But one must work hard to arrive at this particular conclusion, because in a country where the proclamation of freedom of speech is embedded in America's Constitution, and in a world where anyone can don the cloak of religious zeal and say or do anything they wish under this guise, one must be careful to separate the wolves from the shepherds in order to adequately protect the sheep.

I raise this topic of the abuse of religion—and the reactions of certain friends, colleagues, and the public in general to it—because it brings to mind a time when I was faced with something similar, though not nearly as extreme. It involved someone who was very important to me at the time, and still is to an extent. Some years after my relationship with Yolanda Dove, I met a young man named Dana Mallory. The impact he had on my life, part of which is partially covered in my essay *From Here to Eternity*, but I wish to revisit it here for two reasons. One is to discuss how I have come to realize that life is a grand design with lessons to be learned, sometimes from people who enter our lives merely by chance. The second is to clarify the role of religion in my life and to juxtapose it against every other part of my being. Let me preface what is to follow with this statement: in all fairness, I am confident it is never easy for a parent to learn their child is not heterosexual. Even the most loving and understanding parents must suffer a sinking feeling of trepidation, some amount of fear surrounding the good, uncomplicated life they had hoped for their child; one free of unnecessary pain or heartache, ridicule or danger. As it is, life and living can be difficult enough; why stir the pot. And yet here it is, this issue in controversy: sexuality. Something so uniquely ingrained in us all and a topic that even the closest of family and friends can feverishly disagree.

To the point: I was accused by Dana's parents of "making him gay." This came about after Dana had revealed our relationship as lovers to his family. While the Mallory family was always very polite and genial toward me, including me in all family events, they were also very religious. Dana's parents, John and Barbara Mallory, are the patriarch and matriarch of this large tight-knit family. Each has worked hard to build a wonderful life for their six children and multiple grandchildren. Though the Mallory offspring were all taught to embrace the teachings of the church, it seemed at times as if the family's life outside their house of worship conflicted sharply with Mr. and Mrs. Mallory's religious beliefs. What specifically concerned me was their

82

assumption that religion and sexuality (or precisely: any sexuality existing outside of heterosexuality) could not be seen as co-existing. As if all other forms of sexuality were to be considered deviant or abnormal. As if lesbians, gays, bisexuals or transgenders could not be religious, or were anti-God, anti-family, or had some ax to grind against all heterosexuals.

To be honest, up until this issue had been laid at my doorstep I had not given this belief any serious thought. To me, the assumption that homosexuality should be equated with heresy was outlandish and propagated by religious extremists or those who were willfully uneducated about the true nature of sexuality. I had no bone to pick with the Mallory's, but the allegation that I had precipitated Dana's switch to the dark side, made me give my response serious consideration. I had no desire to appear disrespectful; after all, the Mallory's had been nothing short of good to me by welcoming me into their family fold. But I had no desire to appear weak either, as if I had been forced to justify my existence. I had earned my way into manhood and had the bruises to show for it. The trick was this: these were Dana's parents.

Anyone who has been at odds with the parents of a loved one can tell you it is likely a no-win situation. Blood is always thicker. If you stab at the child, the parents come running. If you stab at the parents, the entire family turns against you, partners included. What was worse was that I felt as if I had been thrown under the bus because Dana's protests against this allegation were tepid at best, which left me angered. If this was a representation of our love and commitment to one another, then this example was a poor one. Yes, these were his parents, but at some point a man must be a man and own up to every part of himself, regardless of who approves or disapproves.

Shortly after Dana told his parents about of our relationship, his parents performed an intervention of sorts, flanking him with bibles in hand, reading scripture, invoking God's forgiveness and blessings, and praying for Dana to find the true path of righteousness and right the wrongs of his life. As for me, I was sent greeting cards from the Mallory's, full of scriptures and some damning biblical chapters and verses. While I was initially irked by their assumption that I was living a life of debauchery, never once did I consider turning my back on religion, on faith, on God, on theology because this was the work of Man. When I thought about it from that perspective, I realized it was highly unlikely that Mr. and Mrs. Mallory really knew of many gays, lesbians or bisexuals. That their education on the subject had likely been gathered by what they had seen on television. Mostly news reports featuring gay pride parades that showcased mostly hyper-sexualized near naked men clad in leather outfits or underwear, bare-chested lesbians riding motorcycles and sporting multiple piercings, or effeminate men dressed in the most outlandish women's clothing. They likely had no idea that the vast majority of the LGBT community was not like this at all. For as diverse as the world is, so is this subculture.

I wrote a letter to Dana's mother who, like me, is very opinionated and strong-willed. I never told her this, but I possessed a great deal of respect for her, for the manner in which she managed her family, how protective she was of them, and how much she loved them. For as different as they all appeared from each other, she seemed to love her family equally and totally, and it was to this rational mind that I would appeal. The letter read as follows:

Dear Mrs. Mallory:

I think it imperative to begin putting things back to normal, and that includes the resuming of relationships and the getting on with our lives. It also includes us laying our cards on the table.

As shocking as this may sound, I can sympathize with your dismay at your son's recent admission. While we have had plenty of time to come to terms with how we are, that we are born gay, that we should not feel ashamed or guilty or less than human, we must take into consideration that this is all very new to you. Without education, without understanding, our lives could seem to you an abomination, but I assure you with full certainty our lives are anything but.

Still, as Christians we must allow ourselves to step out of the familiarity and comfort of our own shoes to step into yours and to understand your point of view.

You are a parent, first and foremost. And in a world full of hatred, anger, prejudice and discrimination, the concern you show for your son's safety is warranted. While discrimination is not strictly limited to gays—just the other day someone yelled 'Nigger!' at me—homosexuality is a touchy topic, particularly when viewed through the lens of religion. I could not address that topic with you. Not because I am ignorant of the Bible's teachings, but merely because I have not reached a suitable reconciliation myself. Many churches will always view homosexuality negatively, while those of us who are gay, lesbian or bisexual will always know that we have no choice in the matter; it is part of our DNA.

Those are words that people often do not like to hear: that we were born like this. People like to blame and point fingers, and MANY are under the misconception that we have chosen the way we are. Nothing could be further from the truth. Another misconception is that we are miserable people. We are not. Those that hide and lie often are, yes. Those that move on and lead productive lives do not have that particular problem. Many of us develop a network of friends, because we have one thing in common no matter what our race, sex, age, ethnicity, nationality or religion. It is the one thing that binds us together, because for as much as we may be different from one another, the blanketed hatred displayed against us makes us all one.

86

I cannot describe to you the history of each and every gay person that walks the face of the earth, only that I spent too much time attempting to change what is inherently me and it was impeding the progress of my life and the progress of my relationships with other people. Lies on top of lies to my family and friends had to stop. It wasn't fair to them and it was doubly unfair to me. After I stopped hiding, I felt a heavy burden had been lifted from me. Understandably, it took a very long time before my father and I actually resolved our differences. For a while he blamed himself, feared for my life, was angry with me. Today, we could not be closer. He realized that I had not changed. That I was still his son, as hardworking and stubborn as he.

Again, I cannot speak to you on certain matters where the Bible is concerned. I have no answers for you there. I only know that I am happy, that I have not rejected God, that He remains in my heart and in my life, and that I know of a good deal of religious people, many of whom are gay, lesbian, or bisexual, who believe in God, who are actively religious, and who participate in the church—just like your son. I also know that no one has a special purchase on God's love, and that anyone who is under that impression is seriously mistaken. There is nothing anyone can say that will make me believe that I am not covered by or deserving of God's love and mercy. There is nothing anyone can say to make me eschew God or my religion.

But I get where you are coming from. How you might have reservations about this. Let me tell you: Dana is my best friend, my partner and confidant. He believes in me when I have trouble believing in myself. I realize he would not be a good man if not for his parents. Despite everything, my love and respect for you and your family will not wane. I hope our relationship sees smooth waters soon. And remember this: it is a sad person who equates the definition of being a man or woman by the function of their sexual organs. In my opinion, being a man means so much more and takes so much more. There is intelligence and strength and determination, responsibility and devotion and depth, honesty and love, integrity and character. So many things more. To look at one small section of another person's life, of your own life, is both absurd and insulting. I am much bigger than that and I always will be.

THE AFTERMATH OF me sending that letter was less dramatic than one might have imagined. One: Mrs. Mallory and I had come to an unspoken understanding, a sort of *quid pro quo*. I no more wished to upset her family any more than she likely wished to upset her son. She wanted to protect him. I did too. There was extended mutual respect on those grounds. Furthermore, Mrs. Mallory is a lady, through and through. She is as dignified and respectable as she is forthright and commanding. This could have turned very ugly and it did not in large part, because of her. She allowed me my say, and stood down, if only a little. For

88

this, she will always have my respect. But there was left a topic on the table: this use of religion as a high handed measure to beat down opponents. Things were never really resolved between us. I suspect it will never be resolved between other individuals who find themselves on opposite sides of this divide.

There is something else, however, which leaves a bitter taste in my mouth. For those who feel affronted by the misuse of religion as a sanctimonious lashing, there have come the most unflattering and undignified of responses. Here, the blame has been cast at religion itself, not the actual guilty party: man. For instance, a friend recently posted on his Facebook page a picture of a bible, opened to the First Testament. Beside it he wrote: *As far back as I can remember, I was never really a fan of fiction.* The posting seemed both petty and disrespectful. A colleague of mine, in response to the threat by pastor Terry Jones to burn Qurans, herself threatened to burn The Holy Bible. And for as many gays, lesbians and bisexuals that I know who are God-fearing souls, I also know of a few who have come out vehemently swinging against religion in response to the actions of religious extremists.

Everyone has the right to express him or herself. Some feel as if they have more of a right than others. More still arm themselves either unfairly, unnecessarily, or inappropriately with the wrong weapons, sullying something meant to be uplifting. While others still fire back, confusing the mark entirely. For them, it is okay to toss the baby out with the bathwater. Nothing good can come of this. Not only does one lose access to one's faith (at least on the surface) and falls into the blatant trap of their critic, a chasm now exists between them and solidarity. Another point: with all the hand-slapping, name-calling, and rejection that both sides spend a considerable amount of time engaged in, the good that inherently exists within all of us gets pushed further and further away—until Earth resembles Hell, filled with scorched ground and vacant souls, where no one has God, religion or anything that resembles good in their hearts.

Dana and I are no longer together and I've not spoken to Mrs. Mallory in a very long time. Still, we all exist on the plane of fellowship and goodwill and mutual respect. Not all individuals who have come to disagree in this fashion are fortunate to have arrived at such an understanding—despite our differences. Only the wise keep their relationships valued and in perspective, whether with God or man. Because, in my opinion, we cannot live without either, God or man, no matter how much we proclaim we can.

FROM HERE TO ETERNITY

He knoweth our frame; He remembereth that we are dust.

–Psalm 103:14

I AM A walking contradiction.

I always have been, really. A ball of fire seen as an ice cream cone. A little guy too big for his britches. A ballsy, if insubordinate, warhorse who grew up terrified of *The Exorcist*. A bossy independent in desperate need of human affection. Too black for whites, too white for blacks. An honorary Jew—as one friend calls me—named Hassan. A white man in black skin, says a relative. A Catholic who was once deeply engaged in a homosexual love with a Baptist, says I.

To fully understand my complicated relationship with God, there is something that you will first have to comprehend about me. Because in understanding me, you will better understand God. And while that may sound immediately presumptuous, it is merely to illustrate how big, how beautiful, how forgiving The Creator is. For even after years of rebuking Him in the typical, hypocritical fashion that has been raised to an art form by humans, He saw me as worthwhile enough to send a messenger to save me. The messenger: a handsome young man at a birthday party who would change my life and the way I would look at it, forever.

He would arrive not a minute too soon.

CHILDHOOD WOES

I have always been a contradiction. Born equal parts of diverse parents, my life was and remains a constant struggle between the good and bad parts of each. I grew up in Philadelphia, Pennsylvania no more tragic than any other child who is the product of a broken home. By the time I was 5 years old my parents were separated; by the time I was 8 they were divorced. The battleground that was to be my childhood, that definitively shaped me into who I am today, was fatherless and filled with abuses mental and physical.

I reveal my past not for pity or sympathy, but to point out to you unadorned, no frills, my background and to make a direct correlation to the type of person I would later become: bitter and insecure, defensive and lacking in trust and faith, full of wrath, a lightning rod for arguments that I sought to win at any cost. Like my mother, I humiliated and degraded people, bullying them into submission. Like my father, I became a tale spinner, making up stories about my childhood: to make it seem better than it actually was. I was willing to do anything to rewrite the past, to distance myself away from the pain.

By the time I left home for undergrad, religion was to me then as it had always been during my childhood, something remote-yet-mandatory. Catholicism teaches you order and repetition, and that was the only thing I retained: order and repetition. My relationship with God was as impersonal, as hypocritical, as third-party as it could be. The only thing that I liked about Catholicism was that, unlike Baptist services, the masses were short and to the point, and you could dress any way you wished.

Catholicism has been long-labeled a "beautiful" and "rich" religion. And it was that beauty–the sunlight pouring in through the large, stained-glass church windows; its quiet sanctuary away from the world; the melodic chanting; the ornate candles; the order of the service; the all-powerful, ominous organ that attracted me. Not necessarily God. Not necessarily His message. And like many children of the Catholic faith, all the problems that had plagued me, that continued to haunt me–including chronic depressions, low self-esteem, bitterness, self-loathing, inexplicable anger that I should have given up to God, laid at His altar–stayed with me. These problems governed all of my actions, causing irreversible and instantly regrettable mistakes. Mistakes that I would repeat over and over and over, until I began to hate not only everyone and everything, but also myself. I started to contemplate suicide as the answer to the question that was my life: why go on living if you despise yourself so much? Better yet, why go on living if the person who gave you life despises you so much?

Not once, but three times during the course of my life would I consider suicide–each time coming dangerously close to that final act.

～～～～～～～～～～～

Train up a child in the way he should go: and when he is old, he will not depart from it.
–Proverbs 22:6

THE DARKEST HOURS

Between the ages of 17 and 25, my life darkened blacker than any midnight sky. My relationship with my mother deteriorated to nothing after many unsuccessful attempts to make peace with my past and trust her again–feeling that was the only way I was going to lay to rest the growing dissatisfaction in myself. At every turn she proved me wrong. My brother, caught in the middle of this family dysfunction, moved away to Japan to start his own family. I have seen him only once in the last five years, at our father's funeral. My father and I, despite spending a great deal of our lives apart from one another, came to a truce, much of which is chronicled in my essay *The Acceptance Speech*.

94

Despite this, my life seemed to me a waste, going quickly from bad to worse. Every valuable relationship I had, I destroyed. I kept people at arm's length, not trusting anyone until it dawned on me after I had gotten the wonderful job with the wonderful money and the wonderful apartment, that I was alone, like my mother. The one person I did not want to become. I developed into what she had created: a defensive, angry human being, unable to show affection, cold, distant, and aloof. Or, the most stinging of assessments from any lover: "You're just not a giving person, Hassan."

If they only knew that inside I wanted to give and needed to be loved, but I did not know how or where to start to be the man I always wanted to be. So I fell into a hole called depression. It started with reconfiguring my past in my mind. If this one thing had been different, if only this hadn't happened, I'd be different, I'd be better. But soon enough, after these fantasies came to an end, I'd come crashing down to the hard reality that nothing had changed. The depression eventually crippled me. I couldn't go outside, couldn't eat; I'd miss work for days at a time, not speaking or seeing anyone, I could barely stand the sight of myself. Sometimes I'd slap my face, pull my hair, hating myself. Despondent, I'd wonder, what is wrong with me? And in my mind I'd hear my mother's voice insisting that I was weak, that I was good for nothing just like my father.

It is true what they say about suicide: it's not about causing pain; it's about ending it. Despite many hours of therapy, I came to that conclusion three times. One evening I opened the window to my penthouse apartment and contemplated jumping six stories to my death. I remember that night, feeling all alone, everything so strangely still, as if the entire world was holding its breath, waiting to see if I had the guts to go through with it. True to my upbringing, I second-guessed myself. Instead I sat at the windowsill, crying for hours. Later, in the middle of the night, I was so disgusted with my life I went down to the kitchen and almost slit my wrists with a steak knife. Another time, looking for peace, I nearly swallowed thirty tablets of Demerol—a very strong pain reliever.

Where was God during this time? Not with me, I didn't see him, I didn't feel him. The night after the Demerol incident, I could not stand to be in the house any longer and went for a long walk. I ended up in downtown Philadelphia, near its gay neighborhood. It was there that a black transsexual stopped me on the street.

She looked at me and said, "Honey, what's wrong?"

I looked up at her, not wanting any trouble, not wanting to talk or be bothered. So I shrugged and tried to laugh it off. "Do I look that bad?"

She replied, deadpan: "You look that bad. If you're willing to talk, I'm willing to listen."

And with no place for me to be or to go, I went with her to a bar and had tea. She listened intently as I told her about how I'd tried to take my life. When I was done, she took my hands and told me to pray, right then and right there and I did. Then she told me to go home and pray, and that she would pray for me.

After our talk, we stood and she hugged me tightly, as if she knew that was what my soul was craving. She told me to seek her out if I found myself in trouble again, that the "club kids" knew where to find her. To this day, I credit her with saving my life. And whenever I see her, in a club or on the street in broad daylight, I march myself over to her, and hug, kiss and thank her for being my friend. Thus was the miracle of God working for me. I prayed when I got home for strength, for guidance, for an answer. I prayed the next day. And I got what I prayed for. I found the strength to phone my friends, what few I had. I reached out to them, finding humility, asking for help, love and support. Not long after I felt renewed, like a different person, I felt stronger, more clear headed. I realized that I could leave my awful past in the past and start again, making changes in myself, becoming the person I wanted to be.

I took the good aspects of my father and put them to work. I no longer heeded my mother's words that I was too friendly with people. I went out of my way to make friends and build relationships. I no longer concentrated on the negative aspects of myself. I worked hard on my reinvention, delving seriously into my writing, into publishing, into work, into charity. But in hindsight it was all an act. For as soon as I was better, I forgot all about God. Sending kisses up to Heaven, I proceeded with my life, pretty much without Him.

~~~~~~~~~~~~~~~~

But God said unto him,
Thou fool, this night thy soul shall be required of thee...
–Luke 12:20

LOSING MY RELIGION

One Sunday back in 1992, I was invited to a birthday party in a Philadelphia bar that I almost didn't attend. And there, whether you believe in kismet or not, I fell in love at first sight with a handsome young man named Dana. He was the friend of a friend, from a very religious family I was told, a twin, very sweet and very nice. Under instruction, my friends set out to put us together.

I realize now that what happened to Dana and I was nothing short of a miracle: a love story, a religious awakening, the final chapter in my old life, and the first chapter in my new life. I was reborn. Dana and I dated for the summer months, but the relationship was not to last. He was not out to his very religious family, not serious about his life, and he was an alcoholic. I think I pushed him too far and too fast for a serious relationship, and he fled without a note or a call. This burned me, because I loved him from the moment I laid eyes on him and I realized, as a result of my relationship with my parents, that I suffered from feelings of abandonment. After Dana, I moved on to a series of less than satisfying relationships and sexual encounters that left me exhausted and feeling somewhat cheapened. I finally decided that I'd have sex only when I needed it; that I'd focus solely on work.

When I saw Dana again seven years later, I was a different person. I was no-nonsense and very committed to work. I had a network of friends. I was well respected. I was an uncle, a published author, and I was at the beginning of my journey as a magazine publisher. He came into a bookstore where I worked part-time, and because I tend to hold grudges, I was initially very cold toward him. He asked me to join him and a friend at the club where we first met. I didn't plan on going, but went because another friend insisted. Once there, Dana was determined to engage me in conversation. He talked and I listened for more than two hours, and eventually my feelings for him resurfaced, thawing enough so that by the end of his visit I conceded that he could call me.

Our road to a new relationship was tough. It was difficult for me to get beyond being abandoned by him, as I had come to realize abandonment was a recurring theme in my life. But he held on fast despite my typical boasts of independence; held on like no other lover. This quality struck a chord in me. It was a loyalty I was unaccustomed to, but surely welcomed. This could not have come a minute too soon. For more than a year I had planned to publish an alternative local magazine in Philadelphia. While I felt confident in this pursuit, in January I crashed.

For months I had been preparing to debut my magazine, working endless hours. This meant ceaseless phone calls, visiting clients, managing the staff, editing articles, choosing the cover, writing the opening and closing essays, and so on. Doing all of this while working, while in a new relationship, while getting very little sleep, I soon came to realize that I was running on empty. And then one day I burned out. On the same day that I suffered my meltdown, Dana stopped by unannounced. He said that he came by just to see me and say hello, but looking at me he knew something was wrong. I told him that I could not go on, that I was under so much pressure to do this, to get this right, that I did not think I had the strength to publish the magazine. He asked me if I had talked to God, if I had prayed to Him for strength and guidance. I said no. He said that I should.

He said to me, and I will never forget, that this was not about me and failure; that this was God's way of showing me that I needed Him, that without Him there would be no way that I could proceed or succeed with this project. That this endeavor did not rest on my strength but His, and His will, and that I needed to acknowledge that He was in control, and to rest my burdens with Him. God was leaving me with no other choice but to turn to Him for strength and guidance. No human could help me now, any amount of money. Passage lay squarely with Him.

100

This urge that I had was Him talking to me, telling me that I could do this project, but only with Him, only with His blessing, only with His permission. It was a revelation. I stood there, at once both lost and found, and thoroughly convinced that I had a choice to make and a lifestyle to amend.

~~~~~~~~~~~~~~~~

Though he fall, he shall not be utterly cast down:
for the Lord upholdeth him with his hand.
−Psalm 37:24

GOD'S UNCHANGING HAND

To see your life pass before your eyes is a scary thing. To see it with such clarity, from the moment you are born to the current one, is breathtaking. To have that sight funneled through spiritual awakening, without the assistance of a near-death experience, is simply divine. All at once you realize your place in the world. All at once you can look over your life and see everything that has brought you to the point where you now exist. All at once you understand God's perfect timing. All at once you understand your function in God's plan. You realize through all your hypocrisies that He loved you anyway, that He was there with you anyway, that He spared you, was patient with you, and engineered the perfect plan to bring you right to His doorstep.

101

So it was with me. Sitting and mulling over Dana's words, I realized all that and more. Finally, I could see why my life had been so difficult. It was more than just the building of character; it was a transition to ready me for God's plan, for God's work. I could finally chart my life, my evolution, through incidents that would lead me to this moment, that would mature me and bring me closer to Him than I realized I could ever be. I finally realized that He had spared me from suicide and depression, from abuse and self-loathing, so that I could turn and rest in His arms, so that I could be empowered through Him. I finally realized that I had someone who understood me better than anyone else, who knew my troubles, who had seen me through them, to whom I should have been talking but had chosen not to.

I went on to publish that magazine, realizing the publication would not be the most important thing I would do. There would be more, God willing. And that experience, which felt as difficult as childbirth, was to prepare me for future work. Like Saul on the road to Damascus, the scales fell from my eyes and I was able to see and enjoy all of God's blessings around me. My health, my home, my job, my talent, my friends, my family. Everything was a blessing. God had given me all I ever wanted in my life, had given what fuels me more and better than anger: He had given me love.

Over time, my understanding of God has deepened and continues to grow. And although I remain imperfect, it is the striving in His name that I enjoy. It is the realization that I have been blessed, and so I have a responsibility to be unselfish and pass on my blessings, pass on His word, His lessons to be learned: not to lecture or pontificate or judge. It is the realization that His word is not meant to be a guide for what one should not do, but what one can do. With His love, with His strength, and with His guidance.

But I have prayed for thee, that thy faith fail not:
and when thou art converted, strengthen thy brethren.
–Luke 22:32

HIS EYES ON A SPARROW

When the day comes that I stand before God, I shall be at the crossroads of gratitude. Whom do I have to thank more, thank first: The Message or The Messenger? Do I first thank God for having brought me Dana whom I will love forever, who still knows me better than any other human being–even though we are no longer together–but who inspired me and was there at the beginning of my new life? Or do I thank Dana for bringing me to God, and a peace and purpose and belonging that I think all humans crave and should experience?

I know the answer, and maybe now you do, too. No matter what, on that day, at that hour, at that minute, I will surely be a very lucky man. No, scratch that. I will be a very blessed man.

And I am, I think. I am. Amen for that.

Amen for that.

103

MISSING YOU MISSING ME

I STILL FEEL a connection between us, even though we don't speak. And I cannot figure out why we don't speak; I just know that we don't. I suspect it has something to do with Her. Our mother. And I wish to God this distance between us didn't exist, because I miss you and because I remember a great deal of our past together: good memories, fun times, fights, jealousies, rooms we shared, and then this sort of drifting apart after I left for college which stabs me in the heart every day. I miss you because I love you. You are more than my younger brother. You are my friend.

Do you remember *Cinnamon's Gang*, that comic strip we created when we were little kids–a strip whose characters were named entirely out of things we ate: Spearmint, Doublemint, Nutmeg? I still chuckle to myself about that, and how we would spend hours pretending, with you doing the illustrations and me doing the writing. We even created a pair of superheroes named Blue Flame and Zenith, along with Jason and Andrew (our

Jewish friends from across the street). Do you remember how we would spend hours immersed in comic books? I liked *The Avengers*, *Iron Man*, and *Spider-Man*, and you liked *The Fantastic Four* and *Rom Spaceknight* (who constantly fought against the Dire Wraiths).

From our very early years together back on Tioga Street in Philadelphia, when we were very poor, I remember sitting beside you as we gathered around a hot plate for warmth, eating potato chips for dinner because that was all we could afford. There is a picture of you and me in our grandmother's scrapbook that I look at every time I visit her. The one of us standing side by side inside the hallways of Grover Cleveland Elementary on Halloween; you were dressed as a black cat and I was an astronaut. There are other photos of us: in Atlantic City, with our father, as infants and toddlers of the 1970s. We were always together.

There are other things I think back on. The two of us spending weekends at our other grandmother's house, running up and down Lehigh Avenue with the neighborhood kids during the summer, waiting for the Mr. Softee ice cream truck, rising at 6 a.m. for the cartoons on Saturday mornings, and the first time we discovered a cable channel with the naughty adult films they would show at midnight. I remember our first computer that we programmed in Basic, our love of *Omni Magazine*, your curious attraction to Abba music, and watching *Video Rock* in the mornings. And then there was that stretch of time where we played chess and the violin, on display our competing infatuations: yours of Mozart's energetic body of work, mine of Bach's moody cannon.

I was always very proud of you, and I'm not certain I have ever gotten the opportunity to tell you. I remember when you were living in New York after college and you needed heart surgery. I wondered what life would be like if I lost you and it was almost impossible to imagine. You who were always there, so full of energy, so very smart. I always admired your initiative, your gall, your intellectual and scientific prowess, your hunger to succeed and do anything you set your mind to achieve. I secretly watched in awe, proud as only an older brother could be. I have always thought: *He's going to be fine; nothing is going to stop him.* It may also amaze you to know that I have always thought of you more as a twin than a younger brother. When we were younger we were very different. You were so outgoing as a child, I was sensitive and an introvert. You were like the other side of me, the me I longed to be: liked and loved without condition, accepted and included. You seemed very happy as a boy, and I burned with jealousy at that.

No, this talk would not be complete if I did not mention Her. Our mother. This divide, this topic that separates us. Have you ever noticed that whenever we have talked in the past, that so long as we did not discuss Her our conversations were at their most engaging? I mention this because I recall–almost as if it were punctuation in the commentary of our lives–incidents that separated us, that undermined our relationship as brothers. I think the most stunning were the times you looked at me as if I did not belong in the house, as if I were not your brother but some kid taken in off the street. And I knew it was because of Her. The times you would taunt me with the most hurtful of admissions: that our mother loved you better than me because she told you so. The times when she humiliated me in front of you. I remember at 16 being forced to fully undress in front of you when I came in one evening from doing a school play because she thought I was out doing drugs. I remember a horrific incident when I was ten years old that involved me having to stand in the middle of the living room in nothing but a towel that served as a dress and one of our mother's bras, one hand on my hip and the other limp-wristed, because she suspected I might be gay. You can never know how much pain and humiliation these events caused me for you to see.

You must forgive me for not wanting to mention Her whenever we've been together and talked. But my desire to have a relationship with you–uncontaminated by her influence–was strong. It had already seriously impaired by the relationship with our father. And it devastated and fragmented our family forever. It is why I disinvited Her to our father's funeral. But you...I wish to salvage this relationship with you so very badly, because I remember it from our early years, independent of our sisters.

And while it is difficult to divorce one situation from the other, I wish to start over with you while we still have time, while we are still young, while there are still years ahead of us to enjoy. I do not wish for this to be a complete tragedy.

There is much of you I don't know. I follow your achievements online, but there is nothing more fulfilling than sitting with you face-to-face talking, laughing, and sharing. You have a wife and beautiful son I don't know, and I feel embarrassed that they don't know me. However–and I must be candid here–for this relationship to work, it needs a concentrated effort from you. I have not deliberately kept my distance from you, but I feel that you have from me. Is it Her? Do I remind you of a terrible past? Or have you progressed so far in your life that there is no desire to reach back? I know we don't see eye to eye on the subject of our mother, but is there some way to move beyond that? Being the eldest, I feel like my eyes have seen more than yours on this subject–or at least a different perspective. Honestly, it was bad growing up with Her; hurtful right through to adulthood and beyond. But I do not wish for my relationship with Her to interrupt my relationship with you.

As I've said, I do not wish for this to be a complete tragedy. So whatever you decide, I'll respect it. There are many things in this life that are completely out of our control, but I believe for me much of that time is in the past. I have evolved to believe that you can twist and turn life into anything you desire. That we do not have to accept no for an answer, or accept that life is meant to be a constant timeline of struggling and suffering and regret. That we can step up, step forward, and say: *I survived that and I'm still standing with a smile on my face. I am strong and I'm going to get everything I want out of this life. And if not everything, the most important things.* To me, you are one of the most important things of all.

BUT NOT FOR ME

I'VE EMPLOYED MY fair share of Machiavellian behavior; let's get that out of the way now.

In my love life, I have played villain as much as victim. I have lied, cheated, been indecisive about lovers, been purposefully ambiguous about the direction of a relationship, have slept with individuals solely for the purpose of sex when I knew they wanted more, been cold-hearted, hotheaded, and lukewarm to the most well-intentioned (if ill-executed) of overtures. I have initiated and called off relationships–several times–with a few of my male and female lovers; as if they were my personal yo-yo, interesting one minute and banal the next. My tongue has served as a bullwhip just as much as it has for pleasure. And I cannot speak with any dignity on the times I have kept company with someone I should not have, who belonged to someone else.

I think on those days of my early youth–foraging into manhood with the grace of a bulldozer, sowing my oats wherever I may– with the predictable shame, pity, and healthy heaping of regret that accompanies rearview vision. Why is the road to maturity never easy or uncomplicated? Why does no one really ever tell young people of the true potential and range of their destructive and selfish behaviors? And yet, without the hardships of my evolution, I wonder where I'd be. What lessons would have escaped me? What perspectives would I have on the value of relationships?

This raises another issue altogether: these times, they are a changin'...or have changed considerably since the first time I went on a date. While not everyone travels the same path in life, these days there appears to be a vast number of people who have (with respect to their love lives anyway) steered themselves in a very questionable direction. By this I mean that the dating scene and married life seem almost unrecognizable from the days of my adolescence and puberty, and different even from the turn of the twenty-first century. Some things have remained the same. Men and women still get married and still divorce. Many men still see sex as an avenue to affection, while many women still see affection as an avenue to sex. Some things, of course, have changed. In a growing number of communities across the globe, male and female same-sex couples are now permitted to marry legally. For those same-sex couples who are not legally married, either because their jurisdiction does not permit them to do so or simply because they choose not to marry, same-sex couples are now more public about their relationships than ever.

111

This essay is not about the right for same-sex couples to marry or about the institution of marriage per se, but instead about the institution of relationships and how the mechanics of relationships have changed so much over the years. It is difficult for me to fathom the direction relationships will take in the next twenty, thirty or forty years by mid-century; what they will look like for the generations that follow. While I am confident men and women will continue to get married for as long as the earth spins, I also believe that a day will come that same-sex couples will be afforded the right to marry wherever they choose across the globe, albeit still with some amount of bias and backlash. What concerns me is the mechanics of these relationships, and I often pose a simple question to myself: does a relationship or marriage today (sexes aside) possess the same characteristics of the relationships or marriages of many parents or grandparents? The answer is a swift and definitive NO.

Rarely are there the long courtships of their day, the letter writing to declare unwavering love, and arranged marriages or parental blessings do not have the same stronghold as they once had. Couples can engage in interracial or mixed religion relationships without too much issue, as they once would have in the past. An unmarried woman who is pregnant no longer needs to relocate to hide the pregnancy, nor does she need to marry the father of the baby, nor is she widely considered an outcast if she chooses not to do so. Men and women can end marriages and openly disclose their homosexuality to their spouses and children. Middle-aged couples and seniors are enjoying extended sex lives thanks to the benefits of the women's liberation movement, certain prescription drugs and a greater understanding of sexual mechanics (although there are some pitfalls to be expected with these combined remedies). May/December romances are no longer largely restricted to older gentlemen and ingenues; the Cougar effect is strongly afoot.

Teenagers no longer include First Base, Second Base, or Third Base as part of their lexicon. In fact, they are likely to have the sex their parents never had or will. And they will film it for everyone to see on a webcast worldwide. In some instances, many of today's young people–without fear or shame of public exposure or the ramifications it will have to their futures–become "escorts" or "masseuses" and will either charge or get paid for this pseudo-sexual service that includes performing erotic acts referred to as a "happy ending." This, and more, affects relationships as they have been traditionally viewed and practiced, whether these relationships are opposite sex or same-sex. It has now become somewhat tricky to navigate through a courtship/relationship/marriage because the unpredictable is now commonplace. And as a single person once looking for love, I often think back on times that seem much simpler compared to today's relationship dynamics: such as bearing the stigma of a child from a broken home (as I did when I was younger), or treading the rocky terrain of a divorced parent who takes on a

113

new spouse (as I did after the divorce of my father from my mother).

The reckless, terrible and clumsy years of my evolution into adulthood–a road every young person travels, man or woman–has now been burdened with the evolution of modern times. What was once a difficult period in and of itself for young people (full of first kisses, flirtations, raging hormones, a wobbly self-confidence, sexual awakening and experimentation, losing virginity, confessing deepest emotions, the fresh and scary notion of budding independence and freedom, and first love) is now weighted by the pressures of a world whose boundaries have changed and where anything can and will take place.

I DON'T KNOW exactly what age I was when I discovered that you could see the moon by day, but I remember it made a very big impression on me. It was as if everything I had learned up to that point had been a lie. Well, not exactly a lie (that the moon only comes out at night and hides away by day), but that the adults in my life hadn't been exactly fully forthcoming about all the mysteries of life. These days that mystery involves love relationships, and how mine–in this day and age–strangely wither on the vine, one after the other, not lasting for any significant amount of time, pushing me firmly into the belief that I'm not meant for love and that for all its heartache and tribulations, I may not wish to have anything to do with love at

114

all. Work holds a much greater promise and satisfaction for me at this stage in my life. Or at least that is the religion I have now bought into.

I would title myself in the eyes of romance as old-fashioned, which is funny when juxtaposed against my healthy sexual appetite or sexual fantasies or the reputed way that I "flirt with everyone." In my heart, in my head, I believe in relationships; I always have, even if I failed miserably at them in the beginning. I believe in the happiness relationships bring, in the richness they bestow. I believe in the journey two people can take and the circle of family and friends from a fruitful union. I believe in the hard work to keep it fresh, vibrant, alive, fun, sexy, evolved, and strong. I believe in a progressive functioning of unions in contrast to that era when it seemed that men had carte blanche in relationships (the *Mad Men* era, as I like to call it): behaving as they pleased, their words as law, a good deal of the time existing without regard for anyone else's needs or feelings or sensitivities beyond their own. My father came up in this time and was a good man who cared deeply for his family and was protective of his children. However, I would also candidly admit that he was not the most knowledgeable of the work required to maintain a successful marriage and a well-bonded family. He believed that the work needed to sustain a successful relationship meant that the man actually went to work and brought home a paycheck and nothing more.

115

In those days, a marriage or a relationship was a commitment intended to last a lifetime, but more likely than not turned out to be stressful, a burden, uneasy, uneven, subject to the mores of its time. Marriages and relationships require much work and sacrifice, which could easily be a surprise to the two people involved, particularly if they are immature and inexperienced and became involved at a young age; so it was with my father and mother. Today, there is a lot more information, education and discussion about relationships. Efforts both parties can make to sustain the union, to make it durable–even prosper– throughout the highs and lows, children, families, work, and the constant demands that modern-day living requires of us. Regardless, relationships today also suffer at the hand of time's evolution, of instant and disposable gratification, of I want everything now–and now I don't, of sudden shifting loyalties and fidelities, of associations that don't seem to pan out for any significant amount of time, and that are riddled with secrets and deceit and ulterior motives.

The new way relationships are conducted rankles in stark contrast to the way they were portrayed in my youth. As a child, I was well aware that adult relationships were not perfect; yet, adults seemed intent on projecting the relationship, or family, as solid. Today this is not the case. Many relationships, regardless of the age, origins, sexualities, education, experience or the maturity of its participants, can be publically rocky and fall apart without shame. It is not that the concept of love has changed, only that love today exists during a very tough, cynical and selfish time. Dating and courtship are different, the demands of sex are different, even marriage–which was more romanticized in the past–seems nowadays akin to a contract with a deadline.

In the face of the world we now live in, I see and hear of things that make me more and more disenchanted with modern-day unions. Yes, for the most part, there is a slowly growing, steady progress allowing for people to marry whom they please, love whom they please, have sex with whom they please in any way they please. But with certain advancements–among them technology (which has substantially injected itself into the culture of relationships, one can only assume that the direction of relationships is forever changed. Individuals can now not only trade nude or erotic photos of themselves (with a growing number of traders starting under a legal age), they can also share amateur pornographic videos–recorded all by phone, webcam, or video, to be broadcast on certain web sites for anyone and everyone to see. It is not uncommon to see even married couples broadcasting their sex lives on web sites, the wife or husband sometimes having sex with multiple individuals other than their spouses. Technology (including but not limited to mobile devices, the Internet, and social networking sites on the Internet), has made it that much easier to conduct multiple relationships at one time, or one after the other. Or to acquire or dispose of a relationship quickly or to assume a false or inaccurate identity–

117

which some would accurately argue impacts the ethics of a relationship.

It is not my opinion that technology is bad–or a source of evil or perversion, as some would have the world believe–but that its presence in our lives has had such an impact that our vices are now magnified with these new and growing avenues of communication. The mainstreaming and accessibility of pornography have made it so that anyone and everyone can do it, without shame or stigma, to the point of celebrity. Reality television showcases bad or questionable behavior–again to the point of celebrity–that is often mimicked in everyday relationships. Even email or text communications have deconstructed language and meaningful interaction as we know it. Gone are the days of a simple HELLO, HOW ARE YOU? Now there is SUP, WUT U N2. Fading fast are the days of getting to know someone a little before flirting. Now it is not uncommon for the first line of a communication on a social networking site to contain very explicit and graphic sexual language. People are meeting each other less and less through social events, family, introductions, friendly greetings, or networking. Shrinking are relationships developed out of a simple smile, an accidental conversation, mutual attraction. Growing is the number of web profiles exposing genitalia and private parts before we even get to see a face.

Those searching for love or long-term companionship can find this all very disheartening. Relationships and love seem to have become a crapshoot. Roulette. How can one be totally secure about their partners these days when ethics regarding relationships seem so compromised and flexible? Even meeting someone through a reputable introduction does not guarantee immunity from these perils of modern-day relationships. And so we are left to question: What shall I do; how shall I live? For many, there seem to be two hard choices. Play the game, or stay out of it altogether. For those of us who enjoy meeting new people, dating, looking to marry, start a family, this can be a difficult decision to make. Even if we're not yet ready to settle down but instead wish to explore our options, this can still be a time of risk and chance and disillusionment.

And so that leaves me here thinking that all the lessons I've learned, all the evolution I've experienced, all the things that allegedly make me a catch (that I work hard, am ambitious, fiscally responsible, healthy, respectful, mature), are elements about me that will all go to waste because it seems now highly unlikely that I will find someone with whom I am compatible. As I've said before, I've raised my fair share of hell. I cannot assume to stand on any soapbox. But I worry: about me, about you, about the next generation, and generations to come. I'm worried about all those people out there honestly looking for love. I could tell war stories, horror stories that would earn a scowl from even the most jaded individual. And sometimes I think that for all the things I've done, for all my bad behavior, this is my retribution. Sometimes I think this is just the way that it is for everybody.

Sometimes, however, I do dream about meeting someone and experiencing that moment when everything is perfect. You know how it is: your heart pounds and you cannot wait to feel the electricity of a first touch, the blinding moment of that first kiss, the warmth of laughter, and the thrill and anxiety of starting down a road together. No relationship is perfect I know that. But that sweet moment of initiation, of first hellos, of commitment and years together, then looking back over the fruits of your togetherness, seems to me sometimes as perfect as life can get.

THE BROTHERHOOD

IN THE AUTUMN of 1986, long before I considered living in Washington, D.C., there was a large party being given in the District. Among the attendees was a quartet of men discussing social groups. What was most notable about this assemblage was that each was gay and that one of them was Vernon L. Strickland, III, who would go down in history as being the driving force behind one of America's continuing LGBT legacies. While each of the four had participated in some form of extracurricular activity in college, only Strickland had been a member of a university fraternity. Each man expressed a deep regret over the lack of alternative social organizations during their formative years. They also believed not much had changed in this regard. While there were indeed service and political groups (such as the Log Cabin Republicans, a gay and lesbian federated political institution), Strickland did not believe there were any existing gay and lesbian social groups that did not suffer from internal division or lax membership standards.

From this one conversation there was born Delta Lambda Phi, the oldest-running gay fraternity in the United States. After that initial discussion in late October, one of the gentlemen from the party contacted Strickland in November with an intriguing proposition. If he and his friends supplied the initial funding, would Strickland be willing to create a progressive social fraternity based on the collegiate model. By Strickland's notes on the creation of Delta Lambda Phi, or DLP (as it has come to be affectionately known by its members), he was not sure his partners fully understood the fraternity experience and how much time and work would be involved in undertaking such a task. Yet, by December Strickland had signed on as DLP's trustee. Taking up temporary residence in Georgetown, he started laying the initial groundwork for the organization, which included the selection of the centaur as the fraternity's mascot, designing the crest, and composing the fraternity's rituals.

By the beginning of the New Year, Strickland started making arrangements to recruit the initial Pledge class of Delta Lambda Phi, but there was a hitch. By instruction of the fraternity's financial supporters, Strickland was only allowed to recommend Pledges, not choose them. So began Strickland's outreach efforts to attract worthy candidates, which included DLP's first rush party to be held at Washington, D.C.'s popular but now defunct gay club Tracks. He also placed advertisements in a local community paper and handed out invites at select bars. On

122

February 20, 1987, one hundred and fifty people attended the event, despite the financial committee's failure to show. At a later meeting, the committee was apprised of the successful rush party, from which seventy-five of the one hundred and fifty candidates received a recommendation from Strickland. Thirty-five were eventually selected by the committee and twenty-nine pledged.

At the very start of the Pledge period, however, the organization suffered enormous setbacks. For the second time the financial committee failed to show at an important meeting and checks started to bounce. It had become obvious to Strickland that there wasn't enough capital to keep this organization afloat, and while he remained committed, he decided that it may be time for him to disassociate from DLP. He was faced with three unpleasant options: one, to explain this collapse to the Pledges and let them decide the future of the organization; two, to assume the debts of the fraternity himself; or three, to simply walk away. Surprisingly, the enthusiasm of the Pledges made dissolution of Delta Lambda Phi difficult, and Strickland realized that a very valuable union would be lost. In a bold move, he set up a payment plan with the financial backers of DLP and became the sole and exclusive owner of the fraternity, so that on April 10, 1987, after weeks of a trying Pledge period and initial outing, Delta Lambda Phi welcomed twenty-four men into full Brotherhood. They were the Alpha Chapter of a now legendary organization.

Many years later, in January 2005, the coaxing of my good friend Azuree Salazar brought me to Washington, D.C. The District is a very transient place, which can make dating or meeting new friends there tricky, because residents move in and out of the city very quickly and there are countless new faces with the start and ending of university school semesters. There is also the constant change of political administrations, professionals looking to push ahead their careers at non-profit organizations or within a variety of other professions, military personnel temporarily stationed in the region, and the influx of a good number of immigrants looking for work. While I had met a great deal of people in my first year as a Washingtonian, with a new job and long commute, I didn't have time to make many lasting friendships; and the friends I did make were all very busy with their own professional, academic and social lives.

In the winter of 2006, I was sitting in a restaurant in DuPont Circle reading *MetroWeekly*, the city's LGBT newsmagazine. In its Events listing was a notice for potential applicants to join a social fraternity called Delta Lambda Phi, which centered on building new and lasting friendships. Age was irrelevant, and as a self-labeled "progressive fraternity," so was sexuality; it didn't even seem to matter if anyone interested had been previously

124

part of a college or university fraternity. By the time I read this notice, the organization was in the middle of its rush season and I decided to attend early one Wednesday evening. I enjoyed the initial event and decided to attend another later that week at Georgetown University to meet fraternity leadership and gain further understanding of the organization. There, I was able to read through DLP's history and view countless scrapbooks containing photos of past Pledge classes. The Delta Lambda Phi story was an impressive one and the camaraderie reflected in the photos seemed authentic. There were pictures of trips, parties, community service events, and all of the Brothers I made acquaintance with that day said that they had met friends through the fraternity that they would keep all their lives. More than that, there was a sense of brotherhood that was evident at the event. Everyone seemed to mix comfortably with each other, laughing, telling stories, chatting. I was drawn to this camaraderie and decided I would submit an application for consideration.

Days later I was invited back for the intense interview session for Pledge candidates. The house used for this event was filled with all types of men: different races, ages, looks, backgrounds. The interview, conducted by three pairs of Brothers, was probing. Where was I born? Where did I work? What was my education? What were my strengths? What were my weaknesses? Identify adjectives that could be used to describe me. Would I have the time to dedicate to a Pledge period? Would I be able to take instruction? What did I hope to take

125

away from this experience? When I asked why there were so many questions for a social organization, I was told that they were the ones asking the questions. At that moment all humor left from my face, and I leaned forward and said, "Make no mistake; I ask questions, too." One of the Brothers smiled and the interview was over.

In a week's time I was informed that I'd made the cut; I was to become a Pledge of the Alpha Xi class. On a very cold and icy February evening, I gathered with seven other candidates whose ages ranged from the early twenties to the mid-forties. We were all blindfolded at the meeting location and escorted to the secret induction ceremony. There we took an oath to follow the rules of Delta Lambda Phi, to unite and discover the true meaning of Brotherhood, to find ourselves as men, and to serve the community at large.

THE FOLLOWING TWELVE weeks involved a heavy schedule of events that included weekly Pledge meetings. There we learned the Greek alphabet, the history of Delta Lambda Phi and the history of fraternities in general, the meaning of the fraternity mascot and crest, the general principles of the fraternity and its purpose and rules, and the fraternity song, flower, colors and cheer. We also had the opportunity to introduce ourselves and be introduced to the full body of the organization. There were events we were responsible for planning, meetings with our Big Brothers, tests we had to take, a community service project to

126

complete, a scavenger hunt, a sporting event, a weekend trip away, and a retreat. In other words, to be part of DLP was to truly experience a collegiate fraternity, and this meant long hours in addition to whatever else was going on in our lives. But despite our professions, tiring commutes and extended nights, we Alpha Xi Pledges became family almost immediately.

Call it kismet, but this group of men–a majority of us of the Type A personality–fell in step as if we had known each other for years. Perhaps it was our sense of humor, our defined characters, our diversified histories, the fact that we were so different from one another, or because we related to each other's personal stories. We made each other laugh just as much as we frustrated each other, and before long we began to reach out to each other as actual brothers. Perhaps it was our Pledgemaster who made a great impression on us by acting as a guardian, speaking with each of us at length through any difficulties we experienced–even in our personal lives—and best of all: becoming our most ardent cheerleader and one of the truest friends we would ever have as a collective body.

There were other things that solidified our union: the meetings that forced us to study together and the Pledge tasks to be completed, where we learned about each person's strengths and weaknesses. Toward the end of the Pledge period, there was the Alpha Xi class retreat, a remote event designed to bind us men as a single body with a single working mind. I remember the retreat for a few reasons: some funny, others very sobering. The trip out to the remote ski location, Snow Shoe, in West Virginia resulted in a test of nerves. When we arrived at the retreat cabin at 3 a.m. we drove up on a giant brown bear standing on his hind legs, scavenging through the trash for food. I will never forget the scream that came out of my throat as I thought that this could possibly be the final moments of my life: at the mercy of a huge, hungry and angry bear. Luckily the animal was as afraid of us as we were of him, and he plopped down on all fours and bolted off into the woods. It took at least a solid thirty minutes before any of us got out of our cars.

The remainder of the trip involved exercises meant to bind us together, two of which provided us with profound *Aha!* moments that brought us closer to ourselves and our fellow Pledges. One involved a rope that each of us was given. We were to tie one end of the rope on one wrist and tie the other end of the rope to a fellow Pledge's wrist, so that we were all bound in a giant circle. We could not go anywhere alone for some time, including the bathroom. This time was to be spent talking to one another on any subjects we wished. By the time it was all over, with the laughs and jokes and snarky comments, the exercise managed to melt any lingering ice between us. We were completely at ease with each other and it could be said that we had come to such a point where we could answer in each other's words. It deftly prepared us for the event that night: a baring of souls unlike any of us had ever experienced.

After dinner, we gathered in a circle on the floor by candlelight, Pledges and Brothers together. In a secret ceremony, we told stories about ourselves; stories that could never go further than those involved on this particular night. These were stories that revealed the most painful incidents in our lives. There were tears, long silences, and cracked voices as we disclosed some of the most heart-aching things a man could reveal about himself and his past. I spoke about my fractured relationship with my mother and father. Few people knew the entire embarrassing story, but it felt good to reveal it in this safe space, to let go of that pain, to share this direct correlation between the me of yesterday and the me of today, to share my personal struggle to be a better man. It felt particularly good that I was in the company of men who realized that as men we hold on to far more pain than we should. It was liberating to open my heart and release these haunting memories and let in these men and their goodwill, friendship and love.

When we returned to the city we were all profoundly changed. A deep and meaningful bond had been forged. Outside of a final examination, there was something called a Night of Madness: a party the Pledges throw for the Brotherhood. We went with a Studio 54 themed event (complete with outlandish costumes) that turned out to be an unforgettable night of laughter and hedonism. The last thing we had to complete was the Initiation: an all day/all night exercise where we would be questioned by various members of the Brotherhood on everything we had learned about the fraternity, followed by a final exercise meant to utilize "the one body, one mind" approach, and then the final ceremony where we would be welcomed into full Brotherhood. It was one of the longest and most rewarding days of my life.

I recall a Brother I never particularly cared for jealously stating that the Alpha Xi class would break apart, that our friendships would fragment and drift, that we would disappear from each other's lives. It was a childish statement that could not have been further from the truth. To this day, many years later, we Alpha Xi Brothers of Delta Lambda Phi's Alpha Chapter remain in constant communication with each other, and still gather up for birthdays, dinners, movies, parties and vacations together. We pull together when one of us is in need, even though our lives have taken us in different directions. Although the organization is many years into Vernon Strickland's creation, the benefit of his vision is not lost on us, or on me.

Vernon Strickland created Delta Lambda Phi as more than just an alternative social organization, an outlet of fun and parties. It is a legacy handed down from generation to generation, meant to build men and Brothers and friends. It was meant to help men looking to make meaningful connections with other men, which often does not happen as much as it should. It was initially meant to bring gay men out of the shadows of obscurity, literally and figuratively, and serves now as a reminder of our strength in unity, how walking in another man's shoes–learning from him as he learns from you–benefits a community as a whole. We learned that acceptance and tolerance never grows old, and selflessly serving the world's many communities alongside your Brother is something a man can always be proud of. For me specifically, it was all that and more. My time with Delta Lambda Phi has provided me an insight into myself I would not have otherwise achieved. It has helped me on my evolution in this journey I call manhood, it has opened my heart wider to trust, and it has given me Brothers whom I shall always love and respect, and I know in my head and heart they will always come to my rescue should I ever need them.

I thank Vernon Strickland for this miracle. I am certain there are other Brothers out there who have a tale of their own about the positive and substantive impact Delta Lambda Phi has made on their lives. Even without Mr. Strickland or Delta Lambda Phi, the overall message remains clear: in a world where lines are drawn between *me* and *you*, and *us* and *them*, the best gift we can give our self and the community is to come out of the shadows. We must reach out and build bridges. This is my wish for everyone, but particularly the men and boys of the world, because for us it has always been a bit more difficult to trust, to let go of our hurt and anger, to learn something new. There is no time like the present to become the man you were meant to be, to work alongside your fellow man, and for the good of the world: making your presence known.

131

TIME STOOD STILL

SHOULD HE GET to be old enough, there comes a time in a man's life when he experiences something so unique it defies explanation no matter how proficient he may be with words. Words will never be able to adequately express what it was like to live through a particular ordeal, or to adequately grasp the significance of the moment. He will only understand the emotions and the impact and resonance it had in his life, and pray dearly the words he selects do justice to what happened.

When a man has reached the age where he must rummage through the attic of his mind or heart or both to recall a specific life-changing event, he does so with mixed feelings. He thinks to himself: *God, I remember that,* and all the feelings that are associated with the memory hit him with the force of an ocean wave reminding him of that time, nearly knocking him over if he remembers clearly enough. When I think to myself: *I am still around; I am still here standing*, I breathe a sigh of relief. I thank God. I know I am still here for a reason.

There are a great deal of things across time, specifically within the twentieth and twenty-first centuries that man has seen, where he can be asked, *Where were you when?* Do you remember the First World War; the Second? Can you remember where you were on December 7, 1941? Do you remember Hitler and the Holocaust? Do you remember the American South from any period from the year 1900 forward; do you remember segregation and integration? Do you recall the Red Scare or Drop and Roll or the Atomic Bomb and Hiroshima? Do you remember the excitement over Elvis or The Beatles, Jimi Hendrix or The Stones? What about the cultural shift of The Civil Rights Movement, The Women's Movement, Black Power, the start of The Gay Rights Movement? And then there are the assassinations that rocked America to its very core: President John Fitzgerald Kennedy, his brother presidential hopeful Robert Kennedy, and the Rev. Dr. Martin Luther King, Jr. There was Charles Manson, the Moon landing, Free Love, Vietnam, Deep Throat and Watergate, Nixon's impeachment, Jim Jones and the Guyana tragedy, and the four hundred and forty-four days in which fifty-two Americans were held hostage in Iran. There were the first images of AIDS and its early casualties including a young boy named Ryan White, the explosion of the Space Shuttle *Challenger* against the backdrop of a clear blue Florida sky and the effect it had on American space exploration. Do you remember the video of the beating of African American Rodney King and the acquittal of the four white police officers charged

133

which led to days of rioting in Los Angeles that caused the death of fifty-three people?

Do you remember Operation Desert Storm, the murders of Nicole Brown Simpson and Ronald Goldman? Or the subsequent trial of accused ex-husband and sports legend O.J. Simpson that dredged up, as if from the murkiest swamp, a simmering racial divisiveness in America? Do you remember the near-impeachment of President Bill Clinton, which opened a Pandora's Box on the subjects of decency and privacy and Washington in-fighting. Do you remember September 11, 2001, the first day of the new century that will forever live in infamy? It was a day in a long line of days in our history that would mark the initiation of an unforgettable era. It was seismic shifting of American culture, of global behavior, of a move away from complacency to a time filled with anger, vengeance, scandal and a new vigilant America. And like no time before, this country would never be the same again.

HOW LONG DOES it take for a man to become a patriarch? What are the requirements? How much must he see or experience? Must he be the eldest male member of a family, its core? Must he be embattled or a lion, or filled with tales and lessons he passes down to future generations and from which they must learn? Or can he merely stand like the first inhabitants of the planet and say *I was there; I lived through this...*?

134

With my father's death, as the eldest child I stand at the head of my family. Remembering my personal history there are times when I have felt embattled but in recent years see more and more of the lion in me exposed; I am slowly developing into the patriarch of my immediate family. I have witnessed a great deal in my time. I was just a few months old at the assassination of Martin Luther King, Jr., but I remember watching Watergate coverage televised on the NBC, CBS, and ABC networks. To this day I remember the images of the blindfolded American hostages being held in Iran. I remember the gruesome photographs displayed on nearly every newspaper cover of 912 dead bodies, men, women and children, lying *en masse* from a coerced group suicide on the Guyana campground run by religious cult leader Jim Jones. I remember clearly the impact of the 1986 explosion of the Space Shuttle *Challenger*, televised live largely due to onboard schoolteacher Christa McAuliffe. I also remember terrifying images of the first ravaged AIDS patients: gaunt, dying; the haunting isolation housed in their eyes as they suffered from what the media initially titled "gay cancer."

If there were any defining images from the 1990s, it was that of the videotaped and televised beatings of both Rodney King and truck driver Reginald Denny, only to be outdone by the images of sports great O.J. Simpson fleeing from the police on a Los Angeles highway, a suspect in his ex-wife's brutal slaying.

The Simpson murder trial and its not guilty verdict created in me, and much of the United States, a complex tangle of emotion. I can still recall with unerring clarity the reading of his verdict and the ripple effect it caused across the nation, particularly because Simpson is black and the victims white. I was working at the time in Philadelphia for the law firm Reed Smith and was in a colleague's office as we listened to the verdict on the radio. That we were of different races took a back seat to our confusion over how an adequate verdict could be reached in this case given its inept and seemingly politically motivated criminal investigation, courtroom mishandling, and sensationalist media coverage.

Shortly after one o'clock in the afternoon the verdict was announced and my colleague and I could hear on the other side of his closed office door the stomping and yelling and shouts of glee from the firm's African American employees. It struck at the heart of me as pointedly disrespectful in the wake of the victims' deaths, which tragically appeared to have been largely forgotten in this celebration. The cheering was thunderous throughout the halls of this Republican law firm and it was later reported to me that nearly everyone who thought Simpson was guilty (or largely responsible) shuttered themselves in their offices and were out of sorts for weeks–many of whom fell on the opposite side of a racial divide. For multiple reasons I felt embarrassed and ashamed, as yet again an ugliness woven into the fabric of this country was singled out and highlighted. It appeared as if little gain had been made for racial harmony, which out of this harrowing episode in American history may have seemingly been the most tragic death of all.

The arrival of the millennium brought with it a date and day as recognizable and defining as few before it in American history: Independence Day, Pearl Harbor Day, D-Day, the day President Kennedy was assassinated. There are few days that all Americans can agree on that stand in their minds as unforgettable. For me, one of those days was a beautiful cloudless Tuesday in the autumn of 2001, when time seemed once again to stand still. On this day, history would sear itself indelibly into the world's conscience and for me, September 11– and each subsequent September 11–returns me anxiously to a nightmare of worldwide significance.

I was in New York City that prior weekend on an anniversary trip with Dana Mallory. I had surprised him with tickets to the U.S. Open in Flushing Meadows; he is a big tennis fan and we were both eager to see the matches of Pete Sampras and Lleyton Hewitt, as well as sisters Venus and Serena Williams, who would eventually battle it out for the Women's Singles title that year. It was a celebratory weekend meant to thank Dana for being patient with me that year. I had lost my father the previous November and the months that followed consisted of a depression I didn't think I would overcome. My time with Dana in New York was filled with good weather, good food, lots of

137

tennis, stepping out in Manhattan, and celebrity sightings at nearly all the matches. Donald Trump and ex-wife Ivana Trump were in attendance at the games, as was Jermaine Jackson, Billie Jean King and Chris Tucker. The weekend left us fairly exhausted by the time we returned to Philadelphia that Monday, but very excited and happy to share with everyone all that we had seen. Neither of us ever got the chance, for in an instant the world had changed to one where no one spoke of too much that resembled good news for a very long time.

THE LAST NORMAL moments of September 11 that I can recall were spent watching the *Today* show, as Katie Couric, Matt Lauer and Al Roker stood before an excited crowd outside of Rockefeller Center remarking on the beautiful weather. I left for the office a little after 8:30 a.m. I was working with the in-house legal team for Liberty Mutual Insurance Company at that time and had only to cross Washington Square Park to get to work. I stopped and chatted with the receptionist as I entered, and she informed me that not only was the office's computer network down but that I was late for an impromptu all-hands office meeting. I told her I would likely skip the meeting and settle into the work and mail that awaited me. On my office phone there was a voice mail from Dana asking me to call him right away and when we connected he asked if I had heard that a plane had crashed into one of the World Trade Center towers. I answered that I had not, but immediately thought it must have been a small aircraft, similar to the 1945 bomber plane accident at the Empire State Building. Although that incident could be blamed on dense fog, today's weather was perfect. Dana said he'd heard a report about the accident on *The Howard Stern Show*; I told him I'd check it out and get back to him.

With the network down, the office was without Internet access, so I turned to the KYW news station on my radio. The first words I heard instantly chilled me. An excited broadcaster was almost shouting, "It's like a mad ticker tape parade here in lower Manhattan!" and in my mind's eye I saw a plane smashing into one of those tall buildings and glass, paper and metal cascading to the ground.

I jumped from my chair and ran to the receptionist, asking her if she too had heard of a plane crash in downtown New York City. She said she had not, but made a call to her mother at home to find out. When her mother confirmed that a large airliner had crashed into one of the towers, I bolted to find an office television. I found a colleague with a handheld Sony Watchman. When we turned it to a news channel, we saw the North Tower of the World Trade Center with a large plume of black smoke rising from it. Except it appeared that now both buildings were on fire. And then Katie Couric confirmed that a second plane had struck the South Tower of the Trade Center. I felt my heart skip and stomach tighten when they showed a clip of the plane in a ghostly dark shadow descending, speeding, into the building and the massive explosion that followed. I called Dana to tell him of the news and that I was watching coverage that included aerial views of the buildings and ground views of people running from the site as rescue and fire vehicles rushed to the scene.

The day turned nearly surreal, like something out of a movie, as every network broadcast continued to loop filming of the attack, showing each plane striking the buildings, and with each viewing it seared itself into my heart, into my memory. I thought, *You will not forget this!* There were updates by reporters from every possible angle near the site, and as if the day had not descended far enough into chaos, another report was announced: a plane had slammed into the Pentagon just outside of Washington, D.C. All doubts that this was some crazy coincidence, some awful dream from which I would awake, rapidly vanished. I ran to the office meeting and signaled emphatically for the office manager to step outside. When she did I told her what was going on, then instructed her to tell the firm's lead attorney that the meeting had to be stopped right away; that America was likely under a terrorist attack. And then in what seemed like no time at all, someone was running down one of the hallways saying that another plane had crashed not far from Philadelphia in Shanksville, Pennsylvania.

The office erupted into pandemonium and I raced back to my colleague with the handheld television, as a number of us gathered tightly around him, shoulder to shoulder, elbow to elbow, even standing on the top of desks and chairs, to view the tiny monitor he held in his hands for us to see. We were then instructed to leave the office immediately and go home; many offices around the city were being let out. I phoned Dana to tell him I was leaving for home and that he should as well, but by the time I had gotten across the park and to my apartment I was just in time to witness yet another of the day's disasters. No sooner had I turned on the television set, than I saw the collapse of the South Tower of the World Trade Center. Amid screams of horror, the building disintegrated in a billowing cloud of smoke that seemed nearly alive and hungry in its reach. For as aloof and restrained as I can be, I was powerless to stop the emotions that swept over me. I was awash in loss, because I knew at that moment I had witnessed the death of thousands of innocent people who could not have possibly gotten out of that building in time, of people still in the area of the World Trade Center, and of countless rescue workers who had raced to the scene.

I remember sitting on the sofa, tears climbing from a place I never knew existed inside me. I remember being unable to move for a very long time, and in hindsight I remember a deep silence despite the television's volume being turned up high. I felt this uncanny resemblance in history to the incident on Pearl Harbor (the sneak attack, the fantastic number of casualties, the astounding devastation). And as the North Tower succumbed in

141

the fashion of its twin, I closed my eyes and dropped my head into my hands. I wanted to stop breathing; I wanted to scream with every ounce of anger I had in me at that moment. I have never felt such rage. And the looks on the faces of New Yorkers only magnified the pain that I felt. This tough, wonderful city that is my favorite, had received an undeserved black eye, and I wanted to fight for her, I wanted to defend her honor.

The coverage from that day forward was endless, constant; I didn't turn off the television for days. I watched the various images of the attacks, transfixed: the first plane hitting the North Tower, the hectic aftermath, the hundreds of visible New Yorkers trapped inside the buildings, the mounting death toll, and so many stories of heroism. I listed to the details outlining the planning of the attack, and the heartbreaking stories of the brave airline passengers who fought back until their deaths. The entire country seemed to hold its breath for a very long time, and during that time, that deafening stillness as planes all across the country were grounded. It seemed that not only had time stood still, but we had gone back in time. I remember very clearly the first day planes were allowed to fly again. A test flight was initiated out of JFK Airport in Philadelphia. I heard it fly above my apartment, and I ran outside to watch as it passed overhead; it was the first time I'd heard one in days and it was good to hear that sound again, to push forward.

About a month after the attacks, Dana and I took a trip to New York City. I wanted to see for myself the site formerly known as the World Trade Center, or from that September 11 forward: Ground Zero. I wanted to personally see this piece of history. New York City, even as far north as Times Square, smelled of burned rubber and the charge of electricity. The streets were quiet, the most silent I had ever heard in this 24-hour city. It was as if the entire town was abandoned, or in a state of unprecedented mourning. The walk down to the Financial District was filled with leaflets posted everywhere, pictures of missing persons, their names, their ages, the last time they were seen alive. Various firehouses that had lost personnel had draped across their facades large black sashes, and photographs were displayed as part of makeshift memorials. Everything near the site was closed; and the grounds, cars, buildings, businesses, and streets were covered in a thick layer of ash as if we were in a war zone. Police would only allow pedestrians to get about a block or so close to Ground Zero. But I could see the metal remains of the South Tower jutting up from the earth. To me it looked like a thumbs up that said *I'm still here, I'm still standing; have hope.* I was happy I had come. It reminded me that I was proud to be an American, that I should be grateful for my freedoms, that I should be thankful to the many people who work so hard to ensure that I retain them.

There have been other moments in history since September 11 that have had a significant impact on me. Among them: the war

143

in Iraq, the capture of Saddam Hussein, America's involvement in the Middle East; Hurricane Katrina, the devastation of New Orleans and the Gulf Coast, and the horrific response by government officials. Also the election of America's first African American president; and the placement of only the third woman to the Supreme Court, which spoke significantly on the growing Latino and Hispanic population in the United States. But that day in September changed me, changed America, changed the world, history and time. If Muslims had appeared to exist within the margins of our consciousness, that stopped immediately. If gains were made toward racial harmony, it seemed forgotten as well. For me, it seemed that for each instance that time stands still, anything–good or bad–is possible.

I often wonder what the world would be like without the attack on the World Trade Center. I often wonder, outside of fanatical revenge, what was the point of it all. Was it–like Pearl Harbor, World War II, and The Civil Rights Movement in its time–to birth a new set of issues for America in the twenty-first century? Like anything else that ages, that evolves, what is America and the world around it required to learn? What will we say of this incident forty or fifty years from now? And what will we have learned? Will it be so clear-cut as the megalomania that threatened everyone with the initiation of the Second World War? Most importantly, when will time seem to stand still

144

again? What will be the incident? What issues will we need to address as a people, as individuals?

As I grow older, I realize that time seems to stand still more often now. It's like God tapping us on the shoulder, reminding us to be aware of our surroundings, to stop being so self-centered, so self-contained, unaware of the ramifications of our actions and reactions; there's a need for us to evolve as a people, as a country, as a world. As if He is whispering in our ears, saying *I know this is going to hurt, but you'll come out of this on the other side smarter, wiser, and stronger.* And all you can do is take a deep breath, close your eyes, and let Him guide you through.

Stories continue to emerge from that time. Just recently, I watched a documentary on the survivors from the Marriott Hotel seated at the base of the North Tower. The hotel itself was all but annihilated as the Tower collapsed on top of it. Miraculously guests, including a woman in a wheelchair and her middle-aged mother, emerged from the ruins, from dust and debris to see another tomorrow, a brighter one. Incidents like this remind me that we must rise like the phoenix from the ashes and soar forward with resolve—smarter, stronger, and with renewed faith. Time will outlast us all, but it need not cripple or distort us. We must embrace it for as difficult as that can be, and lest we forget, remember it, for its lessons never grow old. And are often repeated.

MORTALITY

SNEAKERS FOR THE gym? Check. Enough toiletries for the trip? Check. More clothes than I need for six days in California? Definitely call me petty, but I do love my costume changes. Condoms in the unlikely event that I shall need them? Yeah, but how lucky do I ever actually get on vacations? As my mind wanders over a checklist of items I am sure I've forgotten on my way out of town for a much needed summer holiday, I realize something about myself so startling that this epiphany comes about in a sort of backhanded fashion: I love living.

In sharp contrast to a multitude of dulled minds that surrounds me every day, I actually enjoy riding this bull called Life, grasping for more than my eight seconds of glory, defying the bumpy and dangerous ride, and yes: aching to outdo my contemporaries, sidestepping fools and idiots, charging ahead with gritted teeth, blazing forward, fire in my eyes. This realization comes as I am about to travel on one of five flights I will take over the next week: Two on my way to San Francisco, with a quick layover in Memphis; one to The City of Angels; two back home to the nation's capital with a pit stop in Boston. Between one of the two beverage services on the Memphis to SFO leg (Thank God I ate before I boarded the flight; what has become of luxury air travel?), my mind rests on the topic of mortality like one of those magnificent white birds you see on the Animal Planet network: wings out, gliding down, feet gingerly resting upon earth. I am riding a carrier I don't particularly trust; an airline that seems to constantly find itself in the news, crashing into some body of water, suffering some engine mishap, plummeting to Earth as if on some express flight to Hell. It's no wonder their tickets come so cheaply on the Travelocity site. I am not a nervous flyer in the least bit, but I am definitely resting on God's good humor to deliver me safely to The Golden Gate City.

I like living, and despite the ups and downs I have experienced along this peak and valley ride that I call my life, I like the road I am now on. No grass grows beneath my feet; the velocity is just fine. And that is because—as I airbus above the clouds at 35,000 feet—I am fully aware of my purpose in life. I realize what is to be my contribution to this world. I delight in this; I am hungry, I am driven, I feel the power beneath my skin, the blood pumping in my veins. I believe at times that I can bend metal with my mind and that I can see into the future. I am focused; more focused than I have been at any point in my life. And while the journey to this juncture has not all been easy, each of my life's experiences has equipped me well for my endeavors. I am ready to take this leap to test my mettle. I am ready to seize the brass ring. I am ready to puff up, to stand tall as the man I was born to be.

I look out over the clouds that stretch out like cotton candy for as far as the eye can see, and suddenly there is turbulence. Such turbulence that the plane not only shakes up and down but jerks wildly from side to side. The pilot turns on the seat belt sign, and everyone—flight attendants included—is to take their seat and buckle in. For a moment, and not a short one, I think that this plane will fall from the sky. That this carrier, per its infamous reputation, will carry me to my grave in a fiery ball to some field in Kansas. No 'Miracle on the Hudson' headline for me. All last-minute praying and screaming and crying around me, with me going down, entering Heaven and thinking *Shit, I thought I had more time than this! I was just getting to the good part! I was just about ready to rip open my shirt and show the world I'm Superman! To reveal my true identity! That I am no ordinary man! Here is who I am! I am a leader, not a follower! I am a fighter and a visionary! I am a pioneer! Let me have my moment! Let me have my moment to stand and deliver!*

And then the turbulence stops, and the flight continues on without so much as a hiccup. I realize how angry I have become at the thought of a premature death, and I breathe deeply to calm myself. Taking power yoga as part of my daily workout helps me to focus, to live neither in the past nor the future but clearly in the present. During this moment of meditation, it becomes evident to me that it is more than merely the prospect of dying that has upset me. It is dying feeling ordinary. It is dying without fully realizing my dream. It is dying without having left my mark on this world, without executing my purpose. Then I am reminded of so many people around me: the colleagues, the friends, the family members, the fellow commuters. So many of them house a glazed look in their eyes that only people who are fired up can see it. It is a look lacking purpose, a premature death, a plodding through life as a zombie, an ambivalence and lethargy toward life and living. It angers me to see that look in anyone's eyes, children and adults alike. As if they are out of touch with the world around them—most of all its beauty and potential—that they have lived all the life they can live. They have done as much as they can. At the ages of 30, 40, and 50, they are now waiting to die. Bring on the gray hair and extra pounds. Bring on the sexless nights and junk television. Bring on the excursions to Wal-Mart as a highlight to the weekend and the meandering shuffle through life. Bring on misery and depression and discontent and all the pills used to treat them. Bring on the words *safety* and *repetition* and *stagnation* and *death*.

If admirable individuals throughout history have taught us anything, it is that with an unsinkable desire, an iron will, a

149

roaring flame burning from within, anything is possible. Age will never define a person's potential. Labor camps, civil wars, hunger and poverty, slavery and outright injustice, cannot and will not suppress the most determined of souls. These wonderful figures through time have ached to create, to spin this world, and all future notables will find a way to do so as well. Anything short of that is giving up.

After I had arrived in San Francisco to see my brother and his family, he mentioned to me that eighty percent of the world are consumers while only twenty percent are producers. My brother has always been a balance for me, and his perspective—even after nine years of having not seen each other—was exactly what I needed. While we were discussing producers and consumers literally, we were also discussing them figuratively. For producers, he said, the happiness comes from producing; that is where their pleasure is born. He said this in response to a comment I'd made about how people so readily accept the mediocre in themselves, their self-inflicted limitations, and how I wake up in a cold sweat in the middle of the night because I have come up with a new idea I'd like to implement or how I feel like I am wasting time sleeping when I have projects in the queue I want to complete. I said that my greatest happiness comes from work or after I have finished a creation. That I could not imagine how anyone, anywhere, who wanted to be or do something special could just settle and wait to die. How could they go through life, day after day, week after week, year after year, to their death without creating? That everyone, everywhere needs to find their purpose in life, what their job is here on this earth; to find their passion. Finding one's passion makes living—up to the point of your actual death—all the more exciting, meaningful, and full of inspiration and aspiration. Everything, *everything,* becomes different. There is never enough time in the day, the world becomes a figurative playground brimmed with excitement, each heartbeat is a green light to possibility, and one itches, yearns, to be the person they know they are inside. Death and dying become obscure; something that is inevitable, but not the point. There is too much work to do; so much to get done. Each finish line is an excuse to start another race, to best your own record. In the proper light, mortality becomes immortality when you think, *What can I leave here on God's green earth by the time of my passing? How much can I complete? How much good, hope, energy, possibility can I surge off of me?*

I believe that a good deal of people fill their lives with noise that distracts them from finding their passion, their purpose in life—whether intentional or unintentional. Yes, there is pleasure to be had: shopping, long walks, a good book, the laughter of friends and family, making love, playing sports, traveling and vacations, cooking and eating, an afternoon nap, playing with the kids. But there is also the pleasure of discovering your place in the world, in the history of life, on the calendar of time. There is

151

pleasure in stretching your own limits and building a memorial to your life's work. There is pleasure to be had in saying *I created this, I had a hand in making this, I was a part of this movement, I left this for future generations.*

I said to my brother—and he agreed—that perhaps the consumers act as inspiration for the producers, not only in contrast but also as a distinction. Sometimes when the going gets tough, when there are questions or doubts about your purpose in life, when you need a firm kick in the pants or need to be reminded of your gifts, a producer looks to the consumer, at how what he has created has impacted them and his faith and strength are renewed. He wipes his tears away, dust off his pants, and begins his race anew. I think some of the greatest producers out there are athletes, because they inspire us. To watch them during competitions, to see the determination in their eyes, the struggle and focus, and always the eventual emotional breakdown when their dreams and goals are realized, strikes a chord within me. They are kindred spirits. They are to be cheered.

I took a red-eye flight back home to Washington, D.C., this time on a carrier that had a very public issue with cancelling hundreds and hundreds of flights despite its customer-friendly reputation (you really do pick and choose your battles with airlines); however, this trip runs very smoothly, literally and figuratively. No turbulence and the flight crew were very pleasant. There was even some eye candy seated next to me (how lucky can I get?). Death and dying are very far from my mind. In fact, it's been a fantastic vacation. But something itches in me to get back to my world. While I have had a marvelous time in California, like any true producer I want to get back to my work, to my dreams, to creating. It's the sort of sensation that other producers must feel, and I see plenty of them on all levels: teachers, advocates, scientists, politicians, artists, entertainers, writers, entrepreneurs. But then I think of something I saw long before I started on these flights and on this fixation of death and dying and mortality and purpose. I was at a Washington Nationals baseball game with my young nephew and a couple of friends, a month or so earlier. The game was nearly rained out and there was a family exiting in front of me. A mother, a father, and a kid about eight or nine. There they were: the mother carefully helping the father with his rain coat, the father zipping up the child then handing his wife her purse. They all exited holding hands together as they forged into the darkness and thunder and cold rain, moving closely and giggling. They looked truly happy, especially the kid. Producers come in all shapes and sizes, from all corners of the globe, producing all forms of inspiration. And if there were any producers out and about that night, they also included this family. God bless them all with a long and happy life!

PART THREE

SWIMMING TOWARD THE SUN

DANGEROUS GROUND

I OFTEN LIKE to regale with a story that I use to punctuate the differences of yesteryear and the world of today. This story involves my father and my sister Cindy, back when she was 15 and I was 25. I was visiting my father one afternoon when Cindy breezed down the stairs in an ensemble that is not uncommon to see on young teenaged girls today: a denim skirt at least two inches above the knees and a white cotton blouse that was tied in a knot above her navel. This provocative outfit–used to impress her girlfriends and any male admirers as she paraded through the mall–inspired in my father such a bubbling rage that I felt he would pounce on her from the sofa to where she stood at the foot of the staircase some six or seven feet away. He quietly asked her once to change, but she balked. He asked her again (generously, I thought), and she bravely pushed back hard. He then stood like the sun rises: bold and steady and confident. His face was stone but his eyes seemed about to scorch her where she stood. My own eyes darted to hers, hers flashed to me; my gaze fell to the floor. The matter was settled and she went back upstairs to change.

Each of us of a certain age owns a similar story, where we have pushed our limits with adults–or at least we know of someone who has. I mention this as a segue into a recent event involving me and a group of young adults who made me think of that long ago incident with my father and sister. It also makes me think of my own behavior at that age and the behavior of young adults now at the same age, of the rise of adolescent violence, of the adverse climate many young adults face, and of the future of the world in their hands in light of what I am seeing and have experienced. Not so long ago—on a seemingly ordinary Tuesday at the edge of summer and with only a few weeks left in the Washington, D.C. area school year—I was attacked by a gang of teenaged girls during my morning commute to work. Three girls about the age of 16 entered onto a Metro Red Line train, which was to take me only one stop from Chinatown to Metro Center, the busiest of the underground downtown stations in the District. They entered the train behind a young Hispanic male, about 20 or so, and one of the girls–the largest, the ringleader–pushed him hard and screamed, "Say excuse me, *bitch!*" He responded full of fear: "I said I'm sorry."

I witnessed this from behind a young man listening to his iPod, who moved back a bit as the train entered Metro Station to allow me to pass between him and the girls, who were now seated. My

156

messenger bag may have brushed up against the ringleader–I can't be certain–but it was she who pushed and slapped me, yelling at me to excuse myself. I am not nearly as patient as my father and have very little if any tolerance for unruly children (if this is what these girls could kindly be labeled). I turned and leaned into her, myself now very angry. Less than an inch from her face, I hissed, "Do not ever touch me like that ever again." It sparked a battle. She stood with her fingers in my face and barked, "What the fuck you going to do, pussy?" The second girl stood and screamed. "Get out her face, bitch!" The third also stood up and said something. I nearly laughed at their audacity given my temper, given how easily I flare, but these were three teenaged girls, and this was real, nearly surreal in fact.

What was really odd was that no one on the train said or did anything. In fact, it was almost as if nothing was happening. As if I were in this nightmare all alone. The bells chimed for the doors to close, and I realized that if I did not move quickly I would miss the station for my connection. I got off, but the trio of girls followed and circled me on the platform. They pushed me, spat on me, hit me, and called me things I have never been called–even by another man. Still, no commuter moved to assist, to break up this debacle, or even to call the authorities. Everyone went their way without so much as a word.

As the train pulled away I had a sudden and nefarious thought of throwing each of them on the tracks, but instead I yelled at them to shut up–and they did for one single moment. I ordered them to come with me, as I headed to the station manager's office. They followed, screaming profanity all the way. It did not once cross their minds that I could have attacked them, beat them, killed them even, they were that riotous, that oblivious to the consequences of their actions. They were too young to remember Bernie Goetz, the "New York Vigilante" who shot four teenaged boys he accused of attempted robbery on a subway back in 1984. They were too young to know they were not invincible. There were two Metro employees in the station manager's office when I arrived, a man and a woman. The woman was on the phone and I pointed to her; she pointed to me, as if she knew why I was coming. By the time I reached the office door and began explaining what happened, the girls had caught up to continue their assault on me, pushing and shoving me in front of the two managers. I could not help but think that in a different time, in a different place, the circumstances would be very different. What was even stranger was that neither Metro employee did anything to stop it. They stood feet planted and arms at their sides, as if it were an amusing television show. The male employee told me to just ignore them, that the police were on their way. This is an easy thing to say, but not necessarily an easy thing to do when you are being attacked. As the pushing and shoving continued, I retaliated. At some point

158

the female employee invited me into the office until the police arrived some fifteen minutes later.

When the police arrived, the girls fled but were easily caught. The officers took my statement and that of the girls, as well as the statements of the station managers. Oddly enough, I was nearly arrested because the ringleader claimed I'd shoved her. If not for the female station manager stating that I was only defending myself I likely would have been charged with assault. As the ringleader was led away in handcuffs, something profound was borne out of this incident. During my interview, I asked who were these kids? Were they part of a gang? Shouldn't they be on their way to school? And if so, why didn't any of them own a bag, pen, pencil, notebook? Why did the station managers do nothing to stop the assault when it was happening literally in front of them? Why did it take the Metro police so long to arrive at the busiest train station in the city, during a time of year when Washington is traditionally flooded with tourists?

The officer, sweating profusely and way too overweight to be chasing teens, merely shrugged. He asked if I was originally from Washington and I told him that I had only lived in the District a few years. He began to explain that the Washington school system is not the best in the country; so cash poor that many students must share text books on alternate days–and those are the students who show up, who bring a notebook, whose

159

parents care enough to be involved in their children's education. More often than not, many parents weren't. The children were wild, almost savage, exhibiting behavior they'd probably picked up from some reality series like *Charm School*, *Bad Girls' Club*, or *I Love New York*. And of the Metro police: well there's not enough money there either. There are only a certain number of officers for all of the stations in the District, so safety is hit or miss.

As it turned out, the ringleader had a record, truancy violations, was on probation, and was only 16. Friends and colleagues were shocked, but not really surprised, when they heard this story. To them, it was just another day in the world in which we now lived. Some of my neighbors mentioned incidents like mine and we thought back to a time when we feared our parents and respected–to some degree–the authority of adults. If my parents had heard that I was remotely involved in an event like this, I would have prayed the police arrived before they did. Here, four separate teachers have told me that there is a police presence at their schools because a good number of students carry weapons, have records, are in the system, or have some form of behavioral issue.

All in all, in the grand scheme of my life, this was not a big deal for me. And yet it was. What if I were a senior, a tourist, or a lone and quiet student–you know the ones (you hear about them on the news as having been attacked and beaten by a group of other children, or who are doused with lighter fluid and set ablaze by a group of classmates, beaten literally to death in the street midday, bullied to the point of suicide, or gang raped after a high school dance)? This incident with me did not occur on a Friday or Saturday night, when one might expect this sort of incident. This was a Tuesday at 8 a.m. in the nation's capital at the height of rush hour. And this was not a group of teenaged boys; it was a group of girls. I realize that seeded within me now is a concern that has managed to elude me in the past. Perhaps this concern is because of this incident or because I am growing older and can compare incidents past and present. Violence perpetrated by rebellious and angry young adults–which has always been a fact of life and part of every culture–is now more explicit, graphic and brazen; bolder, more creative, and promises further deterioration in our society. If this is even a small segment of the future generation, what hope does the future hold?

Without a doubt, the behavioral issues that cause this particular type of violence and acting out, begins in the home, or if it does not begin in the home, it is neither properly monitored nor identified in the child until it is too late. I think back to the mother who informed reporters that she had no idea her teenaged son possessed an arsenal of high-grade firearms to use on his classmates at Columbine High School on April 20, 1999 in Jefferson County, Colorado. Additionally, if a teenager is living under adverse conditions (an abusive environment, drug or alcohol abuse, etc.) it seems commonplace now only to address the issue *after* a devastating consequence. Yet, despite how many news reports involving growing violence perpetuated by teens, it seems as if the public simply shakes its collective head and changes the channel, or clutches their purses and crosses the street. It seems parents rarely exhibit the concern or control over their children today as in years past. But teachers, counselors and law enforcement cannot be expected to do it all.

The very next week after my Metro incident, I was catching a train to work and in the station were the same trio of girls that accosted me–even the ringleader, despite her arrest. As before, they were loud and obnoxious, without books, and verbally assaulting everyone in their path; everyone moved on as if nothing was wrong. There were no authority figures, no Metro police, or station managers despite what happened just a week earlier. I decided to wait for the next train. One missed day of work–one interruption in my life at the hands of these girls–was enough. But I am not one to let a story like this end without some positive resolution, without some fix. For me it is to behave as a positive role model for all young adults, to pass on good and constructive advice, to offer recourse, support and encouragement to each young adult I come across. Hopefully, all the well-intentioned youths that I mentor will assist in outnumbering all the destructive souls who take a turn down a dark path or find themselves on a slippery slope headed for the dangerous ground of destruction—if not to someone else, assuredly to themselves.

In my most forgiving thoughts I know that young adults by their very nature are loud and rowdy. It's funny at times to see them spreading their wings, searching for their independence, attempting to find their voice, their rhythm, the tempo of their gait. But this world–this violent yet ambivalent one–is not the same as the one I remember from my childhood. I assume I should stop hoping for it to be that way again. It has evolved— or devolved—into something else. It is our duty, as adults, to make the best out of a bad situation, to prevent things from becoming worse. We must do it not for our own self but for the next generation, who stand on the most unsure footing of all.

YOU SAY YOU
WANT A REVOLUTION

THIS COLLECTION OF essays came about as something of an accident. I was moving apartments and in the process of packing I found a box of published and unpublished writings. It was not my intention to write a memoir, but once I'd read through the pieces it was clear that they illustrated an evolution, of the many lessons learned over the course of my life. Some of my evolution came about as the result of divine intervention, redirecting me toward the path I should be traveling in order to fulfill my life's purpose and destiny. Others were self-imposed, an extreme makeover, a reinvention, a taking of stock that needs to occur in our lives every five years or so to serve as a reality check, a figurative shedding of skin which keeps perspectives fresh and goals clearly in sight or takes advantage of prospective opportunities that may otherwise be missed because we are stuck in routine.

This essay returns me to the topic of evolution, because I finished it on National Coming Out Day. For those unaware of the meaning, history and significance of this event, it was founded in 1988 by the late Dr. Robert Eichberg and the late Jean O'Leary as an encouragement for people of all sexual orientations to take a bold step in living proudly and openly, without hypocrisy, without shame, and without fear. This day (October 11 in many countries, October 12 in the United Kingdom) has particular resonance with the gay, lesbian, bisexual and transgender community, as it allows its members to reflect and to shed any imposed guilt or burden to hide. Beyond that it offers an opportunity to stand strongly as our true selves, to coax meaningful, honest, and productive dialogue with family, friends, employers and colleagues, even the world at large, and to be seen not as individuals or a subculture, but as a community of people who hail from every corner of the earth, and represent each sex, every race, age, class, education, nationality, ethnicity, religion, and political party.

The founding of National Coming Out Day came about during a particularly dark period in LGBT history. After the emergence of "Gay Cancer" in 1981, later correctly identified as an acquired immune deficiency that effected men, women and children alike, the LGBT community became a collective voice that spoke louder than ever before. A march on Washington, D.C. was organized for October 11, 1987, prompted in part by the rise of AIDS cases and then United States president Ronald Reagan's public lack of acknowledgment of this epidemic and its devastation. The march drew hundreds of thousands of attendees, perhaps prompting Mr. Eichberg and Ms. O'Leary to mark this day as correspondence to the world that the LGBT community was taking—more than ever before—an opportunity to announce its emancipation from the tomb of silence and the shadows of shame, fear, and invisibility. This day would also mark a milestone in LGBT history, following in the footsteps of the United States gay liberation movement that included pickets led by legendary activist Barbara Gittings, demonstrations at the White House and Philadelphia's Independence Mall from 1965 to 1967; the June 28, 1969 riot that occurred at the Stonewall Inn, specifically involving clashes between The Inn's gay patrons and raiding New York City police officers; the start of Gay Pride parades across the United States in 1970 (then called Gay Liberation or Gay Freedom Parades); the removal of homosexuality as a mental disease from the American Psychiatric Association's *Diagnostic and Statistical Manual* in 1973; and the solidification of assassinated San Francisco City Supervisor Harvey Milk as a martyr for gay rights, the first openly gay individual to be elected to public office in the state of California.

The LGBT community's global visibility increased exponentially following the founding of National Coming Out Day, with many countries around the world discovering themselves in a revolution of sorts, as subjects of gay activism

166

and gay pride, they became increasingly a part of social consciousness through local, national and world media. Political and civil rights advances, as well as conversations domestic and international played themselves out in households the world over and through science, medicine, academia, religion, literature and entertainment. People were now finding it easier to broach the subject of their sexuality within their circles; and many high profile individuals did likewise on the world's stage.

But within this steady advancement came other issues involving equality, namely the rights of gays and lesbians to adopt children, to serve openly in the military, to repeal bans on gay and lesbian partners seeking rights otherwise reserved for heterosexual spouses and families, and the legal right for gays and lesbians to marry. Today many of these issues remain hot topics of debate and discussion, handled with tireless energy and aplomb by many supportive politicians, government officials, public figures, religious leaders, and LGBT activists and their allies all across the world. Step by step, progress continues to be made along these fronts—and yet something remains amiss.

For as much confrontation as the LGBT community receives in the form of overt and veiled discrimination, defamation, slander, libel, inappropriate and inaccurate opinions by pundits, along with misguided allegations of gay agendas, there lay deeper issues *within* the LGBT community that speak to its overall identity. LGBT equality has seen significant strides over the forty years since The Stonewall Riots marked a defining moment

167

in the gay and lesbian liberation movement. For many, this has been a distinct improvement from days of old. For others, this has not been improvement enough; they want more and they want it now. But if history is a teacher, we as its students should know that with every two steps forward, there is inevitably a step backward. While LGBT activists and their allies brave the good fight for the community as a whole, there occupies the same room an eight hundred pound gorilla that does not receive nearly as much attention as it deserves.

For all of our achievement outside of the LGBT community, there exists *within* its walls an inequality with respect to race, ethnicity, sex, gender identification, class, nationality, and sexuality. Those outside the gay and lesbian community tend to see it painted with a broad brush stroke even in this day and age of increased diversity. Without criticism, their vision is limited mostly to what is broadcast on national media, at times what dares to be written in news publications and other periodicals, certainly inflammatory comments made over radio airwaves, on podcasts, and in blogs. Yet, even with all that information—unqualified as some of it assuredly is—there should be made a distinction between a view *of* the gay and lesbian community and a view *into* the gay and lesbian community.

It is my opinion that there will always exist age discrimination, racism, sexism, classism, and homophobia. I also believe that despite efforts for equality there will always be struggles for power and people will always use whatever means necessary to

168

gain advantage over their competition, including playing one or a combination of these cards. The unfortunate truth is that for a people who have off-handedly claimed to be progressive in thinking, these discriminations are as much a part of gay and lesbian culture as any other. The most glaring offense is race because it is a topic that goes largely undiscussed between us— and when it is, it is often coupled with anger and resentment, producing results that could be considered a mixed bag. The overall perception of the LGBT community as young, white, party-loving, hypersexual males is inaccurate. This is not only grossly false, it is also a cliché. It galls many to be faintly included as part of the LGBT community based on this aspect— as if every other race were a secondary consideration or not represented at all. Overwhelmingly, the gay and lesbian representation in mainstream media or entertainment is usually Caucasian.

Although race relations have improved a bit over the last twenty years and appear more inclusive, some disgruntled members of the LGBT community contend that segregation is alive and well. I have been privy to these complaints over the years, with many citing examples that noted a lack of racial and ethnic diversity reflected in LGBT media and entertainment, a racial divide in services provided by LGBT organizations, profiling at gay and lesbian venues, even a rift in celebratory events such as Gay Pride parades (in the wake of feeling marginalized, and apart from many gay pride parades that traditionally take place in or around the month of June, there has been established a separate event titled Gay Black Pride and also a very recent emergence Latino Gay Pride). Before any of this begins to reek of hearsay, I witnessed at a sponsored roundtable discussion on LGBT media an editor of a popular national gay and lesbian newsmagazine respond to an accusation of a lack of racial diversity in his publication with, "The stories just aren't out there." But clearly they are out there. There are gay themed events all over the world, taking place in diverse locations such as the Philippines, Taiwan, Poland, the Netherlands, Russia, Spain, Turkey, Argentina, even Lithuania, Slovenia, Latvia, Bulgaria, Israel, India, and South Africa. Yet here in the United States, a country home to many races, nationalities, and ethnicities, it is rare to witness these races working harmoniously within the LGBT community. Even today it can be startling to witness substantive outreach beyond only Caucasians and African Americans to include Latinos and Hispanics, Asians, South Asians, Native Americans, and other races into the collective LGBT fold.

While the issue of race representation within the community presents itself as constant consternation, the issue of gender is no less important. Lesbians have vocalized dissatisfaction at feeling marginalized not only due to their sex but also due to a chauvinistic pro-male environment within the LGBT community. These opinions are not unfounded, because there is evident a notable chasm (whether intentional or not) between

170

gays and lesbians. There are many gays and lesbians who form lifelong friendships and serve alongside each other in the capacity of activism. Still, a majority of the spotlight shone upon the LGBT community is often cast on gay men as opposed to lesbians. And looking from the inside out, the ratio between gays and lesbians in social circles is quite often unequal, favoring one sex or the other depending on the event. Some would argue that the interests are different between the two sexes, but one could also argue that activism aside should there not be evident a deeper cohesion and inclusion because we are one community.

History, however, tells another story. Immediately following the most pivotal moments of the gay and lesbian liberation movement of the late 1960s, a separatist movement was borne in the early part of the 1970s by women feeling a misogynistic attitude toward them from gay men. Seeking autonomy, they constructed entire societies of women that catered only to their interests, such as businesses, social events, political organizations, and communes and housing. They were under the belief that men were the same everywhere—heterosexual or homosexual—and would never change to include them as equals; therefore, these women would not only create a society to their liking, but would bar interaction with men altogether. Time would shine an unflattering light on this line of thinking by the mid-1980s. After expelling male-to-female trangenders discovered in their midst, further fragmentation occurred when a

171

consensus was drawn that the radical feminist ideology that seemed to govern their society was that of white, middle-classed women and that it failed to take into account the needs of women of color.

The transgendered community (either male-to-female or female-to-male) has, by its own account, received a double slap from both gays and lesbians. It seemed, for a lack of better wording, that no one knew where he or she belonged or fit in. One argument contended that while they were born male and may have transitioned into the opposite sex, they were not technically female—and vice versa. Another argument made plain was that this particular group could classify neither as gay nor lesbian and did not share in the gay and lesbian experience or struggle, an opinion that smacked false in the face of history since The Stonewall Riots in 1969 largely involved transgendered people fighting alongside gays and lesbians for their freedoms and rights. Regardless, transgenders continued to be ostracized from certain circles (such as the Gay Games, which are Olympic-type sporting events that take place in various countries every four years for gay and lesbian athletes and that was initiated in 1982 by Tom Waddell). And until recently transgendered people remained largely unprotected by laws that would bar discrimination based on gender identification, even when gays and lesbians were making strides in that area with respect to sexual orientation. The matter of bisexuals also falls into this gray area of placement and inclusion. To the dismay of

172

bisexuals, a number of heterosexuals and homosexuals agree that even one same-sex experience earns the classification of being gay, and that bisexuality is either a transition period before one comes out as homosexual or that bisexuality is merely a denial of homosexuality. It is also believed that bisexuals are indecisive or confused, and while today bisexuals appear included in LGBT struggles for equality, one could argue that bisexuals—like transgenders—remain on the outer fringes of this community.

Furthermore, as in heterosexual communities the issues of age and class have played out unfavorably in the LGBT community as well. Today's culture places a heavy emphasis on being or looking young, beautiful, and virile, the gay and lesbian community—in and of itself youth-centric—suffers as a whole from a lack of serious discussion on the topic of aging. Gay seniors find it particularly distressing that while there is little to no interaction between younger and older gays and lesbians, there is also little understanding of the issues that concern them and no effort to include them in the community and its activities. For instance, small consideration has been made to the fact that many seniors may be alone, without a partner, without friends close by, and without family sympathetic to their needs or want for involvement. While today there exists on the local level efforts at programming for gay and lesbian seniors (mostly independent groups or proactive LGBT community centers), this movement has yet to catch on successfully throughout the gay and lesbian populace in the United States or abroad.

As for the issue of class: many people, either in or out of the LGBT community, seem to be under the impression that the gay and lesbian community is made up mostly of hedonistic and impeccably dressed, highly educated, well-to-do professionals with much disposable income and who spend a good deal of their time traveling, entertaining, dining out, and enjoying life in general without too much of a care beyond the next cocktail party. For as much as the LGBT community is composed of many races, ethnicities and nationalities, it is also composed of many different socio-economic groups. There are gays and lesbians among the homeless, the hungry, the veterans, the disabled, the single parents, those working multiple jobs at minimum wage, those with limited education, among the immigrants seeking a better life from a third world country, among the farmers and ranch hands, among those living in distressed neighborhoods and depressed communities, existing paycheck-to-paycheck, without insurance, without prospects, with criminal records, as part of gangs, in shelters, in senior housing, and so on. This is a side of the LGBT community that is rarely ever discussed.

THE LGBT COMMUNITY has cried many years for a revolution. I have heard the pleadings for acceptance, the battle cry against discrimination, for a better tomorrow, a better life, a better future, a better present. But we cannot achieve a revolution without an evolution, and evolutions begin internally. While the

174

gay and lesbian community is indeed fragmented, it is not in total disrepair. However, in order to achieve our goals we need unity, cohesion, and inclusiveness. Not as ammunition against detractors, but for the well-being and benefit of the community. It is good that we raise fire against suppression, for our rights and freedoms as human beings, as citizens of the greatest nation in the world. But tending to our own garden ensures that when equality is achieved, it is for the good of all members of this community. And so as the song goes: you say you want a revolution? Well, you know...

THE STORY OF O

SAD BUT TRUE confession: I have always had trouble connecting with new people.

This is not entirely surprising given how pointed and direct I can be a great majority of the time, how reluctant I am to engage someone I've just met with anything more than just a firm handshake, an acknowledging nod, and a dead suspicious silence. Some have incorrectly labeled me as antisocial, but nothing could be further from the truth. I am shy by nature and unabashedly skeptical about everything and everyone, because I am not necessarily a trusting man. On average, it takes days— sometimes weeks—for me to warm up to new people, as I eyeball them, deducing why they are in my life, what angle or advantage they are attempting to employ, or how witty, intelligent or an abundant waste of my time they may be. It is a cynical technique I have developed out of a less than charmed childhood but one that has served me well during my adult life as I sift out the clowns and jokers, players and haters, from those individuals who are truly worth my time and energy.

This brings me indelicately to the subject of Barack Obama. While from my childhood I was taught never to discuss money, religion and politics in public, it seems we now live in an era when anything and everything is discussed. For some it serves as a form of catharsis, but in large part it is due to the advent of sensational publications, talk radio, and reality television, that has given almost anyone wishing it a platform. I wish to discuss Barack Obama, not as propaganda but as a conduit to a phenomenon that I was privileged and thankful to witness.

I was not initially an Obama supporter. With a good number of contestants throwing their hats into the ring prior to the party primaries for the 2008 presidential election, it was imperative for me to hear all of the voices before making my selection for the next Commander in Chief. If we as the United States had learned anything from the years 2000 through 2008 it was that President George W. Bush and his administration proved that elected leadership should never go unchecked and should never be given carte blanche to do whatever it wishes without answering checks and balances. There were a good number of contenders for the presidency at the start. On the Republican side were Governors Jim Gilmore, Mike Huckabee, Mitt Romney, and Tommy Thompson; Senators Sam Brownback, John McCain and Fred Thompson; Representatives Duncan Hunter, Ron Paul, and Tom Tancredo; UN Ambassador Alan Keyes; and former New York Mayor Rudi Giuliani. Among the Democrats stood Representative Dennis Kucinich alongside a bevy of Senators, including Joe Biden, Hillary Clinton, Chris Dodd, John Edwards, Mike Gravel, Barack Obama, and Bill Richardson.

Among all of the televised debates that took place in the years 2007 and 2008, it seemed fairly clear early on that there emerged what some could identify as "fan favorites." On the Republican side, much talk seemed to surround Mitt Romney, Ron Paul and Rudi Guiliani, while among the Democrats Hillary Clinton seemed to lead the pack that included John Edwards and Barack Obama. Due either to lack of support, bad campaign management, scandal, biased or excessive negative media coverage all of the likely Republican nominees and one of the Democratic three fell off. While America had long been positioned to clean house of many Republicans after the Bush II administration (most strongly evidenced in the 2006 mid-term elections), Senator John McCain rose up as a viable contender to either Hillary Clinton or Barack Obama. At that point John Edwards had transitioned from muted to completely silenced amid a brewing scandal that revealed the senator had an extramarital affair with a woman who worked on his campaign, and with whom, it was later alleged, he fathered a child as his wife, the now late Elizabeth Edwards, was battling cancer. This cleared the field for a strong arm contest between Hillary Clinton

178

and Barack Obama, the latter of whom gained significant steam as not only Clinton's campaign battled mounting debt, but also as Obama gained significant endorsements, most notably from media heavyweight Oprah Winfrey as well as representatives from the Kennedy political dynasty, Caroline Kennedy and the now late Senator Ted Kennedy.

Even with such significant support, I was not convinced Obama was ready to be the next President of the United States. If this were a different time–a better time–perhaps I would have come on board sooner; but this was following the George W. Bush presidency and America stood with a very damaged global reputation. The new Commander-in-Chief would have to realize that this presidency would compare to no other. It would be a thankless clean up job requiring equal parts remarkable intelligence, vision, determination, and diplomacy; one that would not push the clock back so that America could forget the previous eight years but move it so far forward that the country felt as if it was making headway *despite* the previous eight years. Also, ever present within the consciousness of the American public was the memory of September 11, ongoing wars in the Middle East, "Mission Accomplished," the mounting loss of military personnel, new brands of terrorism (both home grown and international), Hurricane Katrina, immigration, an astounding deficit. Add to this the countless scandals surrounding the Bush administration that included the subjects of torture, ineffective leaders, and a rapidly growing disconnect with the rhythm and change of a new America that has become much more culturally, religiously, and racially diverse. It had also become much younger and more interconnected through modern technology than anyone thought America could be at the time.

This proved particularly true after Hillary Clinton ended her campaign (despite a large female following) and John McCain chose an unlikely running mate, Governor Sarah Palin from Alaska. While it was not surprising that McCain would choose a female running mate, to capitalize on the Clinton and/or Democratic supporters who remained undecided about backing Obama, criticism of McCain's choice grew louder once it was revealed that little was known about Palin, mostly as the result of a lack of proper vetting. This last minute choosing of the Alaskan governor, who in the eyes of many revealed herself to be more of a liability than an asset to her running mate, proved that McCain as a representative of the Republican party was indeed disconnected from the desires of the American people by what many would call the choosing of someone so obviously ill-prepared for the vice-presidency, or the presidency, should at any time McCain be unable to perform his duties. This would quickly become labeled as "More of the Same" in sharp contrast to the platform of his Democratic competitor: Change We Can Believe In.

My support of Obama was borne during this period. While it was doubtless the Chicago senator was a persuasive orator who was able to galvanize his party with inspirational speeches, his team was also insightful enough to utilize Internet and mobile technology to their advantage by marketing the senator to the young, undecided or disillusioned about how the United States government needed to evolve in order to adequately reflect the wants and needs of the American people. Even if I remained skeptical about his qualifications, it indicated to me that he was at least progressive; it is also likely this move struck a chord with a good portion of America's future generations, who realized Barack Obama was more like them than any other candidate in recent years–or perhaps ever. He was intelligent and well-spoken, he was dapper, adept at social media, he was cool, he was youthful, he was energetic, he was inspirational, he was new by Washington's standards (which gave him the aura of being untainted), he had an elegant wife and beautiful children, and all this started a love affair between him and the American public.

But a charismatic man does not necessarily a good president make. True to form, I remained skeptical and was not fully behind Barack Obama until I looked into his history to find the perspectives he employed in his speeches. Barack Obama was born in Honolulu, Hawaii, the only son to Barack Obama, Sr. of Kenya and Stanley Ann Dunham of Witchita, Kansas, who had met in a Russian language class at the University of Hawaii in

181

1960. His parents married in 1961 and he was born August 4th of that same year. When his parents divorced in 1964, his father returned to Kenya and his mother remarried, this time to an Indonesian student named Lolo Soetoro. The family moved to Indonesia but Obama would return to Hawaii, where he lived until 1979 with his maternal grandparents. He would relocate to Los Angeles and then New York to attend Occidental College and Columbia University respectively. He would enter Harvard Law School in 1988, where he would become editor of the *Harvard Law Review* at the end of his first year and president of the *Review* in his second year, the first African American to fill that role. For the early start of his career he was a director of the Developing Communities Project (a church-based community organization) and an instructor for the Gamaliel Foundation, another community organizing institute. He would go on to lead Project Vote in the state of Illinois (a drive aimed at registering 150,000 African Americans) and serve as a professor of constitutional law at the University of Chicago Law School. Still, his concentration would remain on community building and organizing, serving as a founding member of the board of directors of Public Allies, a board member of the Woods Fund of Chicago, a board member of the Joyce Foundation, the Annenberg Challenge, the Chicago Lawyers' Committee for Civil Rights Under Law, the Center for Neighborhood Technology, and the Lugenia Burns Hope Center.

His political career aside, these accomplishments painted Obama as a man of the people; his award-winning books, *Dreams from My Father* and *The Audacity of Hope*, proved him accessible; his speeches–particularly his landmark keynote address at the 2004 Democratic National Convention–identified him as a definitive person to watch. That he would ascend so far so fast–through his Illinois Senate seating and his U.S. Senate seating–brought about justifiable suspicion. Could this very popular man proficiently lead the country out of one of its worst periods in modern history? Posing this question to myself, I realized that my entire bias against Barack Obama was that he was new, that he did not resemble anything I'd seen before. It was embarrassing how accustomed I had become to what government had to offer, that although I consider myself intelligent I was mentally blocked from someone who was uniquely different from the line of presidents that preceded him. Why should he not have the opportunity to lead America merely because he was not white-haired and middle-aged or had spent more than two decades in politics? What experience he lacked in certain areas, such as foreign policy, he made up for in identifying with his country and stoking a new form of patriotism.

It had been a long time since America felt that a president truly empathized with their personal needs and struggles, as well as our inherent collective patriotic desire to reposition the United

States as a world leader and source of unquestionable pride. It was clear that Barack Obama offered access to that glimmer of hope, that ray of light; that to some extent he reversed the apathy that so many Americans felt toward their government; an apathy that nowadays appears intertwined within the very fabric toward governments the world over. There was the lifting of spirits that served as salve on a wound whose origins seemed rooted to the days following September 11, 2001. Instead of government appearing single-minded in the obsession of its own survival, we as the citizens of this country needed to believe in ourselves again, singly and collectively. Obama challenged politicians to reprioritize their commitments to their constituents and asked that the American people look across their differences and assist in the rebuilding of this great country. When all hands were involved, the United States could not lose but instead grow together, stronger, evolved, and prosperous.

Even among those who may have disagreed with Obama's brand of idealism (admittedly an idealism traditionally generated by the Democratic party), many had to agree that America needed a new outlook, a jumpstart, a pep talk, something, *anything* that served to unify the country. The more Obama spoke–at rallies and town hall meetings–a surge of optimism rose up among the people. I cannot say that I was altogether surprised; the country needed a change. If there was any downside, it was of course the issue of race that was bound to continuously rear its ugly head and perhaps serve as a distraction from key issues. For instance people, some of whom are African American, asked repeatedly if I was registered to vote. Given this important election the question was understandable, yet irksome. On its face, the query appeared innocent; after all I have been registered to vote since I was eighteen. In some instances, it was what the question implied that upset me: that because I am a person of color and Obama is as well, I should show solidarity by voting for him without question. I think it is this sort of narrow thinking that has placed many unqualified politicians in office throughout the history of politics, and while in no way was I unsympathetic to the desire for the United States to elect its first African American president, I only wished for it to be done on merit rather than race. Oddly, my support of Barack Obama had reached a level where I did not wish for his campaign for the presidency to be questioned as a fluke or turn of chance.

Despite the fact that his birthplace would later be questioned in a so-called "birther movement" (designed by opponents to disqualify him as president), Barack Obama became the 44th United States Commander-in-Chief in what was the largest voter turnout in nearly half a century. The reaction to his election was overwhelming as the results were finally announced. Live feed from around the globe was televised, and people in cities everywhere seemed generally relieved and elated. In Washington, D.C. the reaction was riotous. People gathered in front of the White House gates chanting for President Bush to leave that instant. On the popular U Street corridor in Northwest Washington, people came out of their houses, out of bars, out of restaurants to crowd seven straight blocks, where everyone was hugging and kissing and yelling in joy. Less than a mile away and just outside my window people were driving through the streets, hanging out of car windows, honking their horns, parading until well past two in the morning, hooting, screaming *Obama! Obama! Obama!* Not one of them was African American. On television, a reporter stopped a beautiful young Caucasian woman to ask her opinion of the evening, and she turned, her voice quivering, and said, "I can now stand next to my Black brother, my lesbian sister, without fear." The reporter turned to a middle-aged African American man next to her. He had tears streaming down his face and he could barely speak. "I thought it would never happen," he said. "I thought I would never see this day come."

That simple statement had such an impact on me as I listened to Obama's acceptance speech, watching young and old, men and women, and people of every race stand side by side, crying one and all. His words, "We are the ones we have been waiting for. We are the change that we seek." had such resonance with me that I also cried, finally realizing that I too had never thought I would see this day arrive. Not solely because we as a people had elected our first African American president, but because our country had survived such a dark period and had managed to come out of it, hand in hand, ready to reclaim the glory of this nation. At least for today.

I recall attending the inauguration, watching it on closed circuit television from the Dirksen Senate Office Building and seeing Washington, D.C. overrun with millions of people who had come to witness the swearing in of President Barack Obama. That night the entire city seemed to be dressed in tuxes and gowns as they attended various parties. I managed to snag a ticket to the State of Arizona Route 66 Inaugural Ball, where everyone laughed and danced and ate and drank and was merry. There was a sense of brotherhood in the air and many African American men walked with puffed chests and heads held high. We nodded to one another with a gleam in our eyes and a ghost of a smile on our lips. We were proud; very proud.

On my way home, I heard a man blowing a saxophone. The night was frigid, and although exhausted and inebriated from the day's activities, everyone remained very gay, smiling and laughing. The saxophonist was playing "Happy Days Are Here Again" and once again the day felt real but surreal. A page had been turned. One chapter had been concluded and another begun. The very next day I was walking down the street, and out of a car window I heard a radio announcer dedicate a song to the new president. It was the popular 1969 single by Sly & the Family Stone: "Thank You (Falettinme Be Mice Elf Agin)." I smiled all the way to work.

187

In the days that followed his election, I became very impressed with Barack Obama. I am a man who believes in hard work, and it gave me pause to see him immediately take the reins to begin his work on changing the course of the country. His appointments, his press conferences, his visits with foreign leaders, his continued jaunts around the nation, lead me to believe that he did indeed take his position as leader of the free world seriously. And while it remains to be seen if history remembers Barack Obama to be an outstanding and responsible leader of the world, a president of the people, one can say definitely that if anything he gave America hope. At least for a time.

HER

I'M GOING TO tell you a story; it is about my mother. If you know me, you know this tale is unlikely to be pleasant. It is 4 a.m. and seems an appropriate enough time to be undertaking such a ghoulish task. An hour when all should be quiet, peaceful and everything still...except my mind, except my nightmares, except the memories of haunting incidents of years past. Yet, it must be told. I must confront this chapter in my life, ugly as it is, to dissected it, examine it. There is a lesson to be learned here, and it is time for my recovery to begin. I am more than ready now. This era of my personal history has hung above me like a storm cloud for far too long. I am going to tell you this story; it is about my mother. But first I'm going to tell you another story as an introduction, to get us started, and then we'll begin.

ONE SUNDAY ON a gorgeous Memorial Day holiday weekend, I shared a late afternoon lunch with a friend's family.

Immediately after, I had a profound discussion with my friend's 13-year-old nephew Eddy. Eddy's mom is a single mother—an attractive woman—with two boys, Eddy and his younger brother who was about five or six. Both were very intelligent and observant, with lots of energy, very respectful, fun and good-natured. The conversation I had with Eddy involved fathers (his and mine specifically) and hurt (his and mine respectively). Eddy was named after his father as I was after mine. And since we had not known each other very long, I was surprised when our conversation veered from small talk to surprisingly heartfelt confessions.

Eddy is a fairly typical 13-year-old. He is lanky and growing tall with the ghost of his first mustache on the brow of his upper lip. He is a dedicated soccer fan, he has discovered cologne, he is concerned about his hair (of which he has much), his voice is about to change, and he's mentioned a girl he likes. He also loves his family, but you can see in his mannerisms, in his eyes, that his ship is at the dock and ready to set sail for the land of teenagers. My own nephew is about ready to approach this juncture, and I can only smile and knowingly shake my head at this terrain unique to young men. At first, Eddy and I are discussing sports: baseball and football teams, soccer and tennis. We then veer into the topics of exercise and friends, travel and languages (he speaks four). Somehow we land on the subject of family. As it turns out, Eddy's father has—in his words—abandoned him and his mother, an act over which he still harbors

190

resentment. He no longer considers this man his father, and would never refer to him as Dad. Eddy recalled an incident when he was a young boy, where his father promised to come and collect him and never did; in fact he never returned home again after that day. Eddy says that he can no longer remember what his father looks like, but this hurt, this affront, he remembers clearly. I told Eddy that my own father was dead; had died suddenly of a heart attack ten years earlier. And that while our relationship had been difficult, in the end I loved him very much.

It was only when Eddy asked about my mother that I had an epiphany regarding the importance of the conversation we were having. How it made sense. Yes, he was thirteen, but his mind had started mapping his personal history long ago; his heart serving as its compass. It struck me as I looked upon the smooth skin of his young face, his wide, wondrous eyes peering into mine, that he was testing the waters of this conversation, wishing to share but also seeking wisdom and guidance: *My God, he's at that age where he's putting it all together. He's no longer a boy, but not yet a man. He's between here and there. A single road that has led to a fork. And because there is not a male father figure present, he's opening up his true feelings. He's asking about the road he should take going forward. The impetus is his father's leaving, the single most profound incident in his life that could hallmark the rest of his days. Painful as it is, he is*

191

clinging to it. And that could be dangerous if he allows his anger and resentment to saturate him, to define him.

I decided to share. I told Eddy that I had not spoken to my mother in more than sixteen years, and at this he was very surprised. I did not lay out to him the reasons why I no longer spoke to her, but I did explain that she had done something that hurt me very deeply (many things, in fact) and that I chose not to participate in that downward spiral of negativity. I had to escape it. I had to let her go, as difficult as it was. My mother would always be a part of the fabric of my being, but I had to release her in order to evolve into the man I needed to be. Making the resolution to banish her was perhaps one of the most significant, painful and embarrassing chapters in my life. I would no longer have anyone to call mother. And that's a hard conclusion at which to arrive when one comes to realize what mothers are for in the first place. I told Eddy it was important he remember that although his father was no longer present in his life, his mother and brother and family still loved him very, very much. And he should never discount that. He would need them in the days to come, the days when he would need their support, love, guidance and understanding. These gifts should come from our parents, but don't always for one reason or another.

ONE LATE NIGHT recently I was in bed and in the middle of slumber I thought I heard my bedroom doorknob shaking, as if someone were attempting to enter the room. I tried to get up but

I couldn't; I was exhausted from the day and groggy with sleep. On the other side of the door I knew instinctively it was her, as if she were an evil apparition: donned all in white, shaking the doorknob violently, her hands, her fists eager to get to me. I lifted my head from the pillow, bewildered; I called out *Mom?*, wondering how she could be here with me after all these years, after all that pain, after all that distance I attempted to put between us. And like a bomb she burst through the door and I woke with a start, still in the dream. She had landed hard on the floor beside my bed, in my home, in my safe space, dead weight, bound and gagged in ropes, bloodied and surrounded by broken glass. And then I jolted awake again, this time to the sound of the air conditioner and the silence of the night.

For many moments, I could not distinguish the dream within a dream from reality. My heart pounded in my chest as my eyes and ears scanned the room, still, dark and silent. I held my breath, waiting to wake up perhaps a third time, fearing she was reaching for me. The look on her face—as on so many occasions before—angry and with intent to do harm. I thought to myself: *Again? Again, she permeates my life and violates it with her presence? Why can't she go away and stay gone? Why can't I just wish her away for good?* I exhaled wearily and lay down, sinking into the bed, feeling as if I were sinking into the earth. I felt like I was falling into the black abyss of my history, feeling like a child, as I stared at the ceiling for almost an hour, alternatively pensive and angry at a past I could not cleanse from my memory. That was four days ago. My conversation with Eddy was two days ago. Today, I feel particularly motivated to clear my head of my mother, once and for all. There is a reason she continues to inhabit my nightmares, and why she still comes back to me after all these years, unprovoked and unwanted.

I have had nightmares about her for many years. A majority of the time she is chasing me, berating me, or we are together in some symbolic setting: dilapidated housing filled with rats, long and dark corridors that extend for countless miles, or at the house where I spent time as an adolescent and she is hitting me, hurting me, or we are physically fighting or almost coming to blows. Whenever I dream of her, it is assuredly a nightmare; not one dream of her has ever been good. There is a reason for this: my childhood with her was without love. It was a constant trauma; never a moment's rest. I have often wondered how this woman who carried me in her womb for nine months had so little maternal instincts toward me. Why I have never felt that she loved me. From my earliest years I had felt a chasm between us, between a mother and her eldest child, who loved her so very much, but was rejected at every turn. It was as if she blamed me for single-handedly ruining her entire life.

SO HERE IS the story I promised: my mother was young when she had me—seventeen—and I was unplanned. Her father was a Puerto Rican boxer, but through a forced adoption she was separated from her parents and siblings and raised primarily by

194

an African-American woman who was Southern, from Rocky Mount, North Carolina. I have learned recently that while my mother was pregnant with me, my father looked to his mother for advice. My father was young, my mother was younger, they were unmarried and expecting a child; naturally, he was scared. His mother advised him to do what he felt in his heart to be right, so he married my mother shortly after in the church where they'd met, and many years later where his funeral service would be held. I was born in December, a few days after my mother's birthday. My brother arrived two-and-half-years later, but by that time there was already trouble in our family. My parents argued all the time, and my mother and paternal grandmother seemed to hate each other. The marriage itself was already in a downward spiral by the time I was five. My parents' lack of warmth and closeness created an animosity in the family that would last for years to come. There are stories I could tell you about my mother's reckless antics and my father's descent into alcoholism, but let's consider that neither here nor there. In hindsight it's clear to see that they were both too young for marriage, for parenting; that his lifelong bout with alcoholism made it difficult for him to understand her, a woman he truly loved but was so complex he could never decipher her. He was too simple for that; she too crafty and complicated.

My earliest memories of my mother were full of fascination. She was a beautiful woman who'd passed on to me her fiery eyes and high cheekbones. I was enamored of her. Men were always fawning over her. Women too. After the end of her marriage to my father, her chronic bisexuality made for a tense household. All her lovers, male and female, created a wide chasm between us. It was as if her duties as a mother and her life as a lover were never in sync; as if one life had to be more important than the other. It seemed she resented the responsibility of children, especially me, her eldest child who was the spitting image of his father and who was perhaps a constant reminder of their painful past. And while I never felt loved by my mother, I was in love with her. She was beautiful, intelligent, often funny and witty, a talented singer, songwriter and musician, related to famed jazz guitarist Monette Sudler and band leader Joe Sudler. She was also the author of a book of poetry.

But along with all that talent and beauty were a fury, a temper, an irresponsibility and sometimes a sociopathic behavior. Once those dark times started, they quickly took root within the foundation of my family. At the start, there were obvious conflicts between my mother and father, resulting in his estrangement and abandonment of my brother and me. My mother would forge a closer relationship with my brother than she ever would with me; my guess: a difficult birth, one in which my brother survived but his twin did not. They played together, laughed together, went places together, just the two of them. It was as if they existed in a world all their own. From my earliest memories, my mother was always emotionally distant with me. She was mostly ambivalent where I was concerned, but when she wasn't I was the target of a fury that made me feel like I was weak, a fuck up, like I'd never be like her or as good as my brother, like I'd never earn a place in my own family. I always felt like an afterthought. Attention was constantly doted on my brother, her prized son. Because of this I was deeply hurt and jealous. Every time I tried to get physically or emotionally close with my mother I was rebuffed with a chill that should have been reserved only strangers. I am not saying that there was a direct correlation between the hostility between my mother and father and her hostility toward me, but given how much I looked like him I thought it was a plausible conclusion. Still, I was completely unprepared for the intensity of the anger my mother directed at me. I was unprepared for the rage she showed me that resulted in a physical, emotional, and mental abuse that haunts me to this day.

I remember my mother's spitting on me because I was too afraid to pick up a hair brush she had thrown at me; when I finally handed it to her, she viciously spat in my face. I was 7-years-old. I remember being forced to watch the horror film *The Exorcist* when I was 8; an unforgettable incident meant to be a punishment for an act I can no longer even remember. There was the time when I was 9 years old and forced to stand for an hour in the living room in front of the open patio doors for anyone to see, wearing only a towel around my waist and one of my mother's brassieres. She made me stand there, my right hand on my hip and my left hand cocked and limp at the wrist because she suspected I might be gay. When I was 10, she slapped a pile of hardcover schoolbooks on the top of my head because she was upset at an answer I gave her. At 11, she choked me nearly to unconsciousness. At 12, she threw hot tea on me in a public restaurant. By 13, I had endured beatings so severe that it took days for my swellings to subside. By 14, she had constantly belittled any of my endeavors. She would punch and slap me about my face and head for any reason at all, and delighted in demeaning me in front of my family and friends and her lovers. When I was 16, she demanded that I strip naked in the living room in front of my brother for a pointless and fruitless drug search. She would also constantly tell me that she hated my girlfriend. But the absolutely worse thing she did to me in my young adult life was to boycott and prevent my entire family from attending my high school graduation, where I was to receive several monetary scholarships including a full four-year academic scholarship to Temple University, which, ironically enough, was her alma mater.

LET'S GET THIS out of the way now: I was not a perfect child, sassy and spirited are kind words that come to mind, but I was far from rude or disobedient, especially when compared to today's teens. I am not going to cry foul too loudly; every family has its issues, its ups and downs, its quarrels that get out of hand. This story could end here, except that it didn't stop when I left home for university. In fact it began a new era of abuse, which did not only involve me but now expanded to others caught in my mother's orbit.

It started the day after my high school graduation. I was still at odds with my mother for not only missing the ceremony, arguably the most important night in my life up to that point, but also for shutting me down when I tried to dissuade her. And all because a week before graduation I attempted to break up a fight between two friends of mine, Laurence Gray and Lawrence Blakely, that landed us in the principal's office. She used this as the reason behind her punishment. There was to be no further discussion, no hearing me out, no due diligence on the matter. The morning after graduation she entered my room; it could not have been seven o'clock and I was still in bed asleep. There was no good morning, no interest in or questions about my graduation. Instead, she told me that I had a week to find another place to live, then she turned and walked out. Exhausted after living with her and her abuses, I embraced this freedom with mixed emotion. Of course I was hurt at being so callously evicted, but inside I felt that I could finally relax, breath, be myself, smile. I would finally be able to live in peace without all that negativity surrounding me. We hardly said two words to each other for the remaining six days that I was there.

It was that following September when I discovered why she was so eager to get me out. All of my various monetary scholarships, for which I had spent countless hours writing essays, were due to arrive. When I phoned my mother to ask if any of the checks had arrived in the mail, she said no. But a university investigation revealed otherwise, that they had been forged and cashed by a friend of my mother's. Without that money I was penniless and unable to purchase books or supplies. I was forced to find two part-time jobs almost immediately; one to earn cash for school, one for food, rent and clothing. When I confronted my mother about this, she did not deny her involvement. Instead, she looked me squarely in the eyes, defiant, and said: "But you still love me." And she was right; I did. But why did she not love me? Not only had my mother stolen the money I had worked so hard for and lied about it, but she used the fact that I loved her as a weapon against me.

This would not mark the first time I had considered a life independent of her, but was the first time it crossed my mind to make it permanent; to turn, walk away, and never look back. When I allow myself to feel the rage that has lodged itself within my heart I should expect to suffer nightmares. I should expect to come to hate her, and years would pass before I would feel compelled to make things right between us. She is, after all, my mother. Most people hold their mother in high esteem, and I want to as well; to feel pride and dignity at our relationship, no matter what had happened in the past. I was also jealous of the close relationships others have with their mothers, at their shared laughter, warmth and togetherness. I wanted what they had. I wanted a relationship with my mother but she went out of her way to undermine my efforts.

After the scholarship incident, she would contact me only to ask for money, which she never paid back. My calls to her would go unanswered for months until she needed more money. After several of these instances and a stint at a psychiatrist to work through these issues, I decided to give up. How much abuse could one person withstand in the name of love, for the sake of a family that barely existed? It was now clear to me that she had never taken our relationship seriously and never would, while I had taken it too seriously. I had all this love to give and no parent with whom to share it. Specifically, a mother.

The entire situation left me saddened and disgusted about the hand I had been dealt and forced to play. Could I turn my back on my mother, no matter how awful she was? What would become of the relationship with the rest of my family once they found out? What type of person would it make me, to desire to put my own mother out of my life and never turn back? It all sounds easier than it is, but to actually do it took more courage, more strength, than I ever thought I had. In all honesty, I felt marked and tragic. Being without a mother to give me love, emotional support, and parental guidance set me on the path to being a bitter and mistrustful person. Friends advised me to move forward, to construct a family of my own. But no matter how well-intentioned their advice, they didn't fully understand what it was like being without a mother, what that loss outside of death was like. I had a mother who was alive and ambivalent that she had destroyed a family, my family. Having to explain that caused as much pain to me as the events that led up to it. So I ceased all contact, hardly ever mentioning her. That was until she struck again. Only this time the object of her dysfunctional behavior was not me. I then came to realize that through all those years of my childhood I had been living with a monster.

THE THINGS I found out about my mother reaffirmed to me that I made the right decision to put her out of my life for as painful and embarrassing as it has often been. Chief among these revelations is my mother's relationship with my father. I have said it before: my father was a simple man, a good-humored working Joe who was popular among his many friends and relatives. His aspirations did not extend beyond his neighborhood, his family, and the people he knew. He loved my mother, and he told me this not long before he died. But he also admitted that he could never understand her or why she felt it necessary to hurt everyone around her. He was referring specifically to an incident that occurred in the late 1970s, after they had divorced. My mother took out a $25,000 loan in his name and without his knowledge. When she was unable to repay the loan, the company came after my father and garnished his wages. Years later, I questioned my father about why he didn't contest with a lawsuit and he said to me: "It would mean that your mother would go to jail, and I couldn't leave you kids without a mother."

This would not be the end of her duplicity. There would be check-kiting, siphoning off money from friends and relatives that would never be repaid. In later years, I found out more than once that someone had loaned my mother money for which they had never been reimbursed. A now late colleague of mine at a print shop who knew my mother and recognized our shared last name, had loaned her $2,000, which she never repaid. I apologized repeatedly until he begged me to stop. Another was someone with whom she played music. She attempted to open a credit card in his name. He said he knew it was her because she had a habit of misspelling his name. Then there were family members, one of whom was the woman who raised her. Apparently as she suffered, and subsequently died from Alzheimer's, my mother stripped her bank account nearly clean of all her money. And in a final horrible act against her, my mother attended neither the woman's viewing nor her funeral.

When I think about all of this, I ask myself: Why didn't anyone stop her? Why didn't we bring an end to her sociopathic behavior? My guess is that we didn't want to pull the trigger, to make her accountable, to put her away where she could either get help or pay for her crimes. She was family, and we hoped against hope that she would change, but she never did. So we all stayed as far away as we could get from her. The last time I saw her was on an autumn afternoon in 1996 in Philadelphia. I had been lunching with a colleague, and we were on our way back to the office. As we crossed the large intersection of Broad and

Walnut Streets, my colleague turned to me and said: "Who is that woman staring at you?" And without even looking up, I said: "My mother." She asked if I wanted to go back and talk to her, but I did not break my stride. I told her that there was nothing I needed to discuss with my mother. Anything that I had wanted to say to her no longer mattered.

MY MOTHER WROTE an email to me years later, telling me that she reads everything I write, that she loves me. I had neither the will nor desire to respond. I disinvited her to my father's funeral. It would have been too difficult to see her on that day, to have attention distracted from honoring his memory. On the surface, all I felt was numb, like scar. When you run your fingers over it, you can still remember the pain, the cause of injury, the slow road to recovery, but in that spot now the skin is stitched over and dead. The best that you can hope for is that not too many people see the scar and ask about it. The best that you can hope for is that you volunteer the information in your own way, in your safe space, that you are not caught unaware by a question that slaps you across the face like a cold, driving ocean wave. *Hey there; where's your mother? Is she alive? You never talk about her.*

Knowing my mother has not come without its blessings and collateral damage. On the one hand there is the relationship with my brother, which continues to be a work in progress; we remain somewhat divided in our opinions about our mother, how exactly

204

to account for her in our history, where to place her in our lives. Not discussing her seems to be the easiest thing to do. We've moved on with families of our own. Our relationship is an awkward rickety structure that somehow still stands, but I feel compelled to build on it, to not lose another thing to my mother. The relationship with my father, my childhood, was loss enough. But there have been backhanded blessings as well. My childhood made me strong and prepared me for a great many obstacles in life. I am resilient, more so than I ever thought I could be. I am a realist where associations are concerned; if they're not working, they're severed. I fearlessly face down enemies, and I don't entertain fools. I am territorial regarding my happiness, because I will never be a prisoner of another dysfunctional relationship. But all this comes at a price: when you're betrayed by a parent, it kills something inside; a softness is lost, a tenderness dies, a veil is dropped, and the world appears a lot less warm and consoling. It is easy to become jaded, bitter, and cynical.

For a long time now I have felt more alone, abandoned, and angry than words could ever describe. I feel robbed of my childhood, robbed of my parents' love, and pushed out into the world without their guidance and nurturing. But out of this I became a self-reliant and very strong. I was nurtured by the goodwill of strangers and friends, and appreciative that I can still feel love and compassion and humanity in me. Nevertheless, I am always fearful that I will turn out like my mother, monstrous and abusive, reckless and careless with love. But I look at me and my siblings and our love for the family and my fears are abated.

I realize overcoming my childhood was the impetus for me to stand tall and strong, to survive many of life's hardships, a lesson in keeping the faith and remaining focused: on my evolution, on my happiness, and my future. I now know that through the darkest times, leaning on your faith and believing in yourself is invaluable. It taught me that no one, not even your own flesh and blood, not even your mother, should keep you from happiness. Happiness lies within our own hands, to shape, to mold and to develop; all else be damned.

ALL THIS LEADS me back to my young friend Eddy. For some reason young men gravitate toward me for advice. It must be God's way of saying that this is part of my life's work, part of my life's purpose. I feel good about this, particularly after having been made to feel worthless for so long. Eddy and I will continue to talk, and I'll pass along to him these bits of wisdom to let him know that someone is on his side, that someone knows his pain, that someone he knows has survived. Recently, Eddy saw his uncle hitting his 13-year-old cousin with a belt because she forgot to wash his clothes; his wife did nothing to stop him. Eddy later told his mother that he was happy he didn't have a father in his life, that he didn't want one. How awful to know he felt this way, but he was shaking, obviously still traumatized by witnessing his cousin's beating. I thought: When do adults forget what it's like to be a child; how impressionable they are? Why don't they see what I see in their eyes: a need for independence, a budding personality, their need for guidance and protection and love? Why don't they see their need to be understood and accepted and nurtured? How could anyone bring themselves to harm a child, to abuse them and their trust? How could they tarnish their innocence and sully their childhood? It not only creates young adults who are emotionally scarred, it births a legacy of abuse, it fragments the family, and could lead to destructive behavior.

I had a friend many years ago. She was French, had lived through World War II, and would often tell me stories about the Germans invading Paris, how she could still hear in her dreams the stomping march of Hitler's army as they passed through the Champs Elysees. She told me her brother-in-law, a Jewish publisher of an underground newspaper, suddenly disappeared after their arrival, never to be seen or heard from again. This woman often called me *sympathique*, the French word for nice or sweet. She asked me how I got that way, and I told her I didn't know. After everything that has happened in my life, it is a wonder to me at times that I am not an alcoholic, a drug abuser, or a raving lunatic. It amazes me that I am strong, levelheaded, *sympathique*. It is God's blessing through and through, I suppose. And the only thing I can think of as I sit remembering my childhood, my heart broken as I retread this scorched earth, the morning sun rising and illuminating the summer sky, is that I'm happy to be alive, to be able to pass along to you this tale of suffering and personal triumph, of darkness and light, of hell and hope. I'm happy to be able to tell you to never give up, never give in, to nothing and no one. Instead, find your faith, your purpose, and allow them to get you through the tough times. Godspeed.

SWIMMING TOWARD THE SUN

"GENTLEMEN!"

The year was 1982. The city was Philadelphia, Pennsylvania. Ronald Reagan was president and I was a newly minted teenager at the not-so-tender age of 13.

He yelled: "Gentlemen!"

For clarification, the person speaking was an instructor I had in high school, who one day in the middle of class yelled this at the top of his lungs. He said the word gentlemen because it was an all boys school, Roman Catholic High School to be exact, erected in 1890 and which still sits on the corner of Broad and Vine Streets near downtown Philadelphia. Television and radio broadcaster as well as legendary NFL Film narrator Jon Facenda attended Roman. Pulitzer prize winner Charles Fuller went there as well. He wrote *A Soldier's Play*, but most people know *A Soldier's Story*, the movie adaptation with Harold E. Rollins, Jr.,

Adolf Caesar, and Denzel Washington before Denzel Washington became a bona fide star and won two Academy Awards.

My instructor, whose name I cannot recall, screamed at the top of his lungs, "Gentlemen!" He had this look and boy I'll never forget it. His skin was normally pasty like curd, like one of those singers out of a barbershop quartet, but not today. This day, this hour, his face was hotter than an Arizona heat wave in August. And it was titled back and away, the way an angry housewife looks at her husband when he stumbles through the front door after midnight, three sheets to the wind and smelling of whiskey, cigarette smoke, and—if he got lucky that night— the perfume of some young, pretty thing who looked like she stepped right out of the pages of a *Sports Illustrated* swimsuit magazine. He bellowed, "Gentlemen!" and his eyes burned in his head. He said to us boys, wild and rowdy: "Do you know the difference between paradise and a prison?"

Now because we were in biology class at the time we all thought this was a trick question. The room, which had up until that point been swelling steadily in chatter as our instructor was attempting in vain to explain the proper dissection of a frog, suddenly fell silent. Each of us looked to the left and looked to the right, and realizing we were all lost with this question...well, we just stayed silent. There in the room sat twenty or so boys— at or about the age of 13—quiet as church mice; to be heard only the Broad Street traffic outside. Jesus Christ himself could have walked into the room at that moment and no one would have batted an eyelash. That's the way we were back in those days when an adult raised their voice. Not like that too much anymore. Most of the boys in the class—in the school, when I think about it—were Italian from South Philadelphia, some African American from the north side of the city, a few Chinese out of Chinatown, a Greek here or there, a scattering of Irish and Poles. We dressed in uniforms back then: navy blue or camel colored V-neck sweaters with the Trojan emblem on the left tit, collared shirts, dress slacks, and polished shoes always. Anything less than that and you were sent home with demerits. Too many demerits and you were sent home with a suspension. Too many suspensions and you were looking at public school and two very angry parents. My instructor yelled: "Gentlemen! Do you know the difference between paradise and a prison?" And when no one could answer his question, he said: "A visionary and a fool."

Now it took me a long time to figure that one out, but when I got it I got it. And let me tell you, before I did I spent a whole lot of time searching for my paradise and a whole lot of time trying to escape this prison called my life.

SO HERE IT is: the greatest lesson I have ever learned. And this is especially for all the young rabbits out there still working their way out of the hutch for the first time. You know how it is. Seems like you can't move this way or that without someone telling you you're making a mistake. You can't say this word or that without somebody saying that you're wrong. For all of you, I have some good news and some bad. Bad news first. *You will never please all of the people all of the time!* No truer words were spoken. For any opinion you have there will always be some undignified, self-righteous, obnoxious asshole who will say to you that you're wrong. And as far as assholes go, they'll probably be the loudest one in the crowd. For any move you make in life, there will assuredly be some critic who will solicit to you their unwanted opinion that not only have you fucked up, but that they could have done what you did twenty times better in their sleep at 3 a.m. Here's the good news: the rightfully revered Eleanor Roosevelt once said, "No one can make you feel inferior without your consent." Let that sink in for a moment and you'll get my point.

Finding your lot in life, finding your tempo, your heart's desire, your home, whatever you want to call it: it's hard. Recognizing it is even harder. Getting others to appreciate it is almost impossible. But that's life. It's a long swim upstream, against the tide, across the English Channel. But my friends, once you find your stride, once you hit it, nothing, not the dark night, not the distracting voices, not the naysayers, pocket players, or petty day players should steer you from your course. But first you've got to find it. And I guess that's what we're here to talk about today. Living, it ain't easy. And finding yourself, finding your calling, is one of the hardest jobs you'll ever have. Staying true to yourself, staying true to that calling, that's the second hardest. And I'm not sure that anybody had a harder time at those two vocations than me.

You see, I was not the kind of guy who was lucky right off the bat in terms of knowing who I was or how my life was going to turn out. I wasn't a pretty boy, no rich man's son, no family business, no connections, and growing up with my mother was hell. But what the hey, we all have our crosses to bear. What I did know was this: that despite my questionable upbringing I wasn't a half bad-looking fellow, I had smarts, could turn a phrase, get a laugh, had lots of energy, sharp as a tack, looked good in clothes, and I didn't do bad in the dating department. I knew something else as well: I didn't necessarily fit in anywhere. I was what the old timers would politely call "One of a Kind." That was good and bad. Good because I never ran with a crowd. Bad because I never got invited to run with a crowd. My senior year high school English teacher wrote me a note just before graduation, which sums up a lot about my life. It read: *Dear Hassan: To be one of the avant garde means extra rewards, as well as extra suffering. But...a man's reach should exceed his grasp, else what's a heaven for? You will never be ordinary, so don't bother trying. Follow your bent; be true to yourself; let small people snicker and whisper. Hold your head up, and never let them know you hurt. It won't be a rose garden, but it will be worth it. Sincerely, AB.* I still have that note from Arlene Bernstein. God bless her heart for shining a prophetic

213

light on this rocky road called Life for a near-sighted traveler like me.

SO LET'S GET down to brass tacks: I started my career of One of a Kind fairly early. To borrow a phrase: picture it: Philadelphia, 1972. I am four years old. My beloved first grade teacher Miss Campbell—a looker by the standards of those days with her long blonde hair cascading down on each shoulder, she in a suggestive pink blouse and a lovely pleated white skirt that barely kissed her kneecaps—informed her students that we were to prepare for our first gym class the following week. Boys were to wear white crew neck undershirts and a pair of white shorts and sneakers. Girls were to wear their one piece God-knows-what-color-blue-this-is gym outfit. The next week comes. Girls were to get changed in the large coat closet to the right of the room, boys in the classroom itself. This was back when you could do such a thing in the public school system. Definitely not that way anymore. When we were done, we were to form two lines at the front of the class: boys to the right shortest to tallest, girls to the left shortest to tallest.

If ever there was a smacked-ass, it was me. Why? Because when Miss Campbell said that the boys were to wear shorts, I thought she meant underwear. So there I was descending the Samuel J. Clemens Elementary School main staircase toward the gymnasium, my bare skinny ass in a pair of tighty-whitey Fruit of the Loom underwear, tops and bottoms, with red, white and

214

blue tube socks and a pair of Bobos. For those who don't know what Bobos are, allow me to educate you: they are cheap sneakers kids wore back in the 1970s, two steps below Pro Keds but not quite walking barefoot. I don't know why they called them Bobos, except to me it didn't sound all that far off from Hobo's. Go figure. The neighborhood children used to tease if you wore them. They'd sing: "Bobos, they make your feet feel fine. Bobos, they cost a dollar ninety-nine." Yes, I was poor. Hell, most of us were back then growing up in blue collar Philadelphia next to the Tastykake factory and the Budd Auto Plant in Hunting Park. To the amusement of the entire school I was forced to return upstairs to the class and change back into my street clothes, and for weeks the kids teased me about that. I was shut out of certain circles, laughed at both to my face and behind my back. My detractors should have stuck around for more.

Fourth grade, circa 1974. We used to play a game at recess called Catch a Girl, where all the boys chased after all the girls in the schoolyard. One day I was invited to play this game and I yelled out to a buddy of mine after the chase began, "What are we supposed to do when we catch the girl?" My friend—whom I considered close—yelled back over his shoulder, over what sounded like a megaphone, "KISS HER, STUPID!" No one ever accused me of being a sharp knife.

Autumn, 1982. Roman Catholic High School. Teenaged boys in the locker room changing after showering being...you guessed

215

it...teenaged boys. By this I mean that most of us by this time had a little peach fuzz on our upper lips, a little peach fuzz under our arms, and—count them!—two pubic hairs to rub together which gave us the right to call ourselves men. Some guy looks up from the locker next to me and yells out: "Anybody got any lotion?" And almost on cue a sinister voice answers back from the far end of the locker room: "Yeah, I got some grey lotion for you if you want it!" Everyone laughs, me included. Dumbass that I was, I had no idea what the hell they were talking about. Who knew that a 13-year-old was required to know what sperm looked like? Again...not so much like that today.

Philadelphia again, 1983. Renee Shindler, the daughter of my geometry teacher stops by my house one day to announce to me that she, along with her father and twin sister, are moving away to North Carolina. So that you can picture this in your mind: Renee Shindler would be considered by today's standards "a hottie." She was a beautiful thing with a gorgeous body, small waist, full *chichas*, stunning eyes, smile, lips, everything. We stood in the threshold of my doorway so that my mother couldn't hear, but that her father—who had brought her to my house— could keep an eye on us. She had obviously wanted to see me and had asked her father to bring her by. She told me she was leaving, and after we had passed through all the small talk she took a step toward me. Feeling that she was maybe invading my personal space, I took a step back. She took another step toward me. I took a step back. She took another step forward. I took

216

another step back and I bumped up against the wall behind me. She leaned in, her *chichas* fully on my chest, and she gave me my first kiss on the lips. One of the best kisses I've ever had in my life. So much so that I remember it thirty years later. It was a long kiss...or so it seemed. My heart was racing so fast, I felt like I was going to faint. She said good-bye after a moment and walked away, stopping on the stairs to look back at me, as though she were expecting something. When I didn't move, she continued down the stairs and I never saw her again. I was a fool. I realized too late—after she had driven away with her father—that I had failed to ask her for her phone number or her new address. I failed to realize that she really did like me, enough to come to my house and kiss me.

Yes, my friends, I was late to the party. It seemed like I was always late to the party. Hell, unlike most boys I had no working knowledge of what masturbation was until I was 19 and unlike most boys I had no idea how to operate the mechanics of sex with another human being until I was 21. Even then to the most lenient of judges, my efforts were questionable. Yes, I had a habit of being late to the party, which left me feeling— understandably—more out of the loop than in. Childhood was a definite bust.

OK, SO LET'S fast forward. Now I'm an adult. Things have got to be better as an adult, right? I'm a big boy now, wearing big boy clothes. No more tighty-whitey Fruit of the Loom underwear for me. I'm the cat's meow. I'm wearing Nautica suits, Italian shoes, designer shirts, ties, cologne. I'm dressing the part to fit in. It's important to me that I fit in, because so much of my life has been spent not fitting in. And get this: because I am an ambitious fellow, I figured I would try to fit in in an area that would do my ego the most good: romance. Try not to laugh, I said I was ambitious.

Now because I am a Sagittarian, I come equipped with something of an ego. Not quite as self-involved as Leos can be, but not as self-destructive as Aries. I mention this, because in full disclosure: Sagittarians love having sex, anytime, anywhere, though not necessarily with *anyone*. We leave that to you Pisces out there. But we Sagittarians are game for sex anytime and anywhere. If you have only fifteen minutes to spare, let me check my book and I'll see if I can fit you in. Personally, I'm an afternoon delight man but hey...I've never turned down evening shade either. The more aerobic the sex, the better; the timid need not apply. For those fit enough, Sagittarians are often open to the idea of repeat engagements despite our reputations as being something of a Casanova.

So here I am on the prowl. I should have known from the start this wasn't going to be a walk in the park. No matter what anyone says, bisexuality does not necessarily endear you to either camp. Most men think you're confused or in denial and most women think you're a jerk. Trying to pass myself off as an entirely heterosexual male turned out to be a laughable endeavor

218

despite all the girlfriends I've had, and I've had a few. My first major relationship was with Yolanda, my high school sweetheart, though I would not necessarily hit her up today for any ringing endorsements. All the rest of my relationships with women ran hot and cold. In their defense I was never fully there and as a result, I came off looking like a heel.

As far as the guys went: I was a little more in tune with them, mostly because I know my own sex. The women got it right, however: we men are screw-ups, and men are as hurtful with men as they are with women. The games, the ambiguity, the indecision, the wandering eye, the laser focus on sex and nothing more does indeed after a while get fucking tiring. I'd be retired to the Virgin Islands if I had a damned dollar for every time I got my heart broken, or every time I felt like I would put my fist through a wall, or every time I felt like pushing some jerk off a bridge. But, of course, that's the way dice roll. As a result I've dated the dull and boring, the sex-crazed maniacs, the narcissists, the alcoholics, the beautiful, the not so beautiful, the airheads, the hunks, the jackasses, the crass, the crackpots, the desperate, and you know what? I could never find happiness with any of them, men or women: the crazies, the vain, the cheaters, the spoiled brats, the one-night stands. It was all a waste of time. Or maybe not. Because I realized what I was looking for they didn't have and never would.

My ticket to fitting in was not with any of these people and it didn't do my ego one damned bit of good. I can say this: in my quest to fit in, I never stepped in any quicksand. No drugs of any kind. I had an alcoholic father, so I was never a big fan of too much drinking. And I had asthma as a kid, so I never took up smoking…cigarettes or anything else. But like my father, I did have a talent for making friends. There's just one problem with making friends. They have lives too. And friends, like anything else in this world, come and go. They move. They pair up. Marry. Have kids. And if you're like me, you eventually find your life a series of evolving dynamics, in which you fit in only for a time and then it's on to a new group of people, some new storyline, some new dynamic to which you must acclimate. That's not to say I didn't have some good friends. I've had some great friends in my time. You name a state and I have a friend there; you name a country, I probably have a friend there too. Or at least a friend of a friend.

It's just that all this left me with an answer that I would soon recognize as my one true love in life: work. The great actress Bette Davis once said about work: "It has been my experience that one cannot, in any shape or form, depend on human relations for lasting reward. It is only work that truly satisfies." Since I am currently without children, I am inclined to agree in part. I have come to realize that work is like a drug; for the ambitious, for me: addictive. There is a reason for this. With work, you don't necessarily have to fit in, only to figure out. To create. While work can often be based on collaboration, it is more often a singular pursuit. In other words, I had spent so much time trying to fit in with other people that I had forgotten to fit in with the one person that mattered most, me. It was there, inside, where I would find my happiness. It was within me where I would find my purpose and a place where I would always belong. There, in the endless discovery of myself, is where I would be constantly entertained, perpetually challenged, always loved, always amazed at what I could do. It reminded me of a saying by the seventeenth century Spanish philosopher Baltasar Gracian, writer of one of the best books ever written: *The Art of Worldly Wisdom*. He said simply, "Don't belong so much to others that you stop belonging to yourself." Because of my childhood I had forgotten to belong to myself. I had forgotten to put me first and in doing so my happiness has always been elusive.

This doesn't mean that I don't need love or friends or family. God knows I do! But when we see our purpose, our reason for living, it becomes like a vision, like a golden, entrancing horizon. And if we're smart, we will keep this destination in our sights. As good friend and former colleague Jim Villa would often say to me: "One foot in front of the other, Hassan." Or to mix metaphors: keep swimming toward the sun that serves as a beacon, as inspiration, as a source of energy, as a reminder that for as much as inspiration can come from outside ourselves, it must also come from within. And it will if we just focus and listen. Too often we surround ourselves with noise, distractions that prevent us from looking within for answers that are readily available, for the laughter that we need, the salve for a wound, the quiet for meditation, the key that unlocks the door to our destiny. We tend to look to others, other things, other situations, and this may steer us off of a path that we are meant to travel. Perhaps there is a reason I was not meant to fit in with certain groups, with certain people. Perhaps it is God's will that I should be focused on a purpose, my more singular purpose, and this may be the reason why I am so happy with working, with creating. Put more succinctly by first century Jewish religious leader Hillel: "If I am not for myself, who is for me? And when I am for myself, what am I? And if not now, when?"

SO NOW AS I ring the curtain down on this bittersweet walk down memory lane, I am reminded of all the things in my past that are forever changed. Samuel J. Clemens Elementary School is long since demolished. I despise tighty-whitey underwear. Roman Catholic High School, its building now considered an historic landmark, was nearly closed in the mid-1980s. And Philadelphia, Pennsylvania—the place of my birth, the place of my upbringing—and everything I have come to know, everything that once populated my memory about the city I once called home, has vanished. The old neighborhoods where I grew up, places I frequented as a youth, streets with familiar landmarks, the bond of community I once shared with a number of friends throughout my adulthood exist now only in my memory. The girlfriends, the boyfriends, the apartments, the

222

places of employment. And what is replaced is a land that is as foreign to me as a place I've never visited. This demonstrates to me that life goes on. And that fitting in for the sake of fitting in is like wearing someone else's clothes, or living someone else's life.

I too have changed considerably since the days of my youth. But a certain part of me remains the same, as if—God forbid—I should lose all my worldly possessions, things would not change for me too much. Because this house called my soul would remain intact. And my vision remains fixed on the sun in front of me. Yes, I see the beauty of the burnt orange sky. I see the ocean glistening like millions of diamonds. I see the birds in the distance soaring high on the wind. And I am remotely aware of the coming night with its twinkling stars, and where I shall sleep peacefully one last time. But most of all, I see the sun on the horizon. Big. Bold. Bright. Magnificent. And for the life of me, I will not take my eyes off of that wonder for anything ever again.

PATRIARCH

MY HIGH SCHOOL English teacher Arlene Bernstein explained to us students one day that men in life, as in literature, face four types of battles: man versus man, man versus God, man versus machine, and man versus himself. Despite everything I have shared in this book there exists no crystal ball that will prepare a man for being a man. Each man's life is his own, is special and unique. This information is merely a reference manual, mine specifically, to remind me of the forward direction in which I am headed, to remember keenly the road that I have traveled. It is true–and I should know–that man is doomed to repeat the history that he has failed to learn. And despite all the battles a man will face in his life, the best point of reference he will ever have is himself and his conscience.

Most of all, this book is a celebration of sorts. I always enjoy being a man. There are things we do that are distinct and unique from our female counterparts; funny things, outrageous and stupid and predictable and amazing, but assuredly us, assuredly male. When we come together and talk and share our experiences, we learn, and we are able to pass on to those coming behind us valuable advice that makes this journey in life a little easier. While the essays in this book are meant for men of all ages, not all of it will apply to every man. There will be men who have other effective and productive ways of confronting the challenges a man faces, of living life well, of being the best man he can be. And this is good. There is no one path to becoming a gentleman, only that a man should strive to be one–and any man can be one, regardless of race, ethnicity, class, nationality, sexuality, socio-economic or educational background. At any point in his life a man can begin the process of becoming a gentleman.

What is most important is that a man loves and respects himself enough to believe this is possible. Without that he will fail. He must believe that there is in him something unique, powerful and aching to be released; an evolved self so determined and shining that he can face any crisis–and with work and faith–prevail. He can dream and achieve beyond the previous generation, can seek inspiration and be an inspiration, he can make the most of his life, simple or complex, and be proud of the life he has lived, and of the good he has created.

I REMEMBER THE summer I was 13 when I had my first "change of life" (to borrow a term). Men get these at various

225

points (during adolescence, after a change of lifestyle, after marriage or fatherhood, experiencing a death, meeting the love of their lives, or at pivotal ages like 30, 40, or 50). Men hit personal milestones that profoundly change their perspectives, and they realize their lives will never be the same again. During this particular change of life I became a man. Oh, yes, I was still young, naive, full of myself, petrified, yet motivated and focused, but skeptical about my life to come. What precipitated this change from boy to young man was a lack of attention and love at home. School became a refuge. Teachers were attracted to my desire to be in class, to soak up as much knowledge as possible, because I was sure education was empowerment and the key to having a better life, to get out of my home, to hit the ground running.

I would wake at 6 a.m. every morning and be in my trigonometry prep class by 7 a.m. I would walk through Chinatown to school covered in the orange glow of the rising sun, thinking, plotting my next steps, remembering what my prep teacher Ruth Shiloh would always tell us students: perseverance is the key; she wrote this in my yearbook as well just before graduation. In some corners of the world a kid my age would be carrying a rifle, or milking a cow, or going to work instead of school, but I was merely trying to survive growing up in a house full of anger. I knew I was sensitive, thin-skinned, hungry for love that never came and ignorant of why it didn't.

One Saturday I passed a used bookstore called Rusakoffs. It still stands today in downtown Philadelphia with kind and gentle owners who play classical music and play chess and gossip with the neighbors of Washington Square West. It was here that I found a book titled *Looking Good: A Guide for Men* by Charles Hix, with photography by Bruce Weber and illustrations by Kas Sable. It was written in 1977 but I didn't pick it up until 1983; the book had long been out of print. Between this and outdated copies of *Gentleman's Quarterly* magazine, I managed to educate myself–as much as possible–on what a man should look like, how he should compose himself, what skills he should acquire to shine the brightest in his circles. While this was "self-medication," I was desperate to be the man I knew I could be. For the most part it worked, and everything else I learned came at the hands of mentors who taught me to shine, to speak well, to stand straight and walk tall, to cloak my fear, to learn as much as I could, to put myself out into the world, and to have faith in myself.

When I was 26 a colleague of mine named Ira Lefton took me aside and told me that while he liked me, he thought I needed to smooth out the rough edges of my personality. Yes, that hurt. But the further away I got from that day, the more I realized that manhood was not a destination but a road, an ongoing evolution. Since that time other friends have said certain things to me, sometimes flattering, other times not so flattering. All of those things have helped me to grow as a man. To realize my fullest potential. To grow bigger than I initially imagined. I see myself very clearly now. I know my faults and shortcomings, but also my strengths. I still seek out advice from mentors, still stretch and grow vigorously. I never want to be bored with myself. I want to be classic.

Truthfully, part of me likes being the center of attention. Not the star player in the forefront, but the one in the background who is often the most valuable player. The one against whom all odds were placed, the one that nearly everyone overlooked or dismissed–and who came forward with faith, determination, will, smarts and vision to close the game. In all honesty I owe a great deal to those who have always believed in me, who whispered encouraging words in my ear, who saw in me what I could not see initially: that shine, that promise, to be a great man, no matter what I did in life. I too have placed a bet on me. I too believe in my promise, in my future, that I have something to contribute to the world, something to say. I realize now that all the work I have done to become a gentleman is the same work that all gentlemen do. I am proud of my efforts to be in their company.

Although there are men in the world who we like or dislike, who are admirable or wretched, great or despicable, we are all brothers in the league of men. Look at the face of each man you pass and you will see what I mean. At one time we were all little boys running without a care in the world, the world around us a vast, scary place full of excitement and things to know and do.

228

In our minds possibilities were endless and we enjoyed this time in our lives. Now that we are men the world may seem smaller, less optimistic, its luster tarnished. This is where gentlemen, true gentlemen, will rise and lead. To make this world, their world, their lives and the lives of generations behind them, better. However, the work will start with you in the swim to your greatness. Take every opportunity to be a great man; in your home, in your family, in your community, in your life. But most certainly in your head and heart.

Swim.

DISCUSSION QUESTIONS

1. How has the relationship you shared with either or both your parents shaped how you presently conduct your life? By word or deed, what was the best advice or course of action you received from either of your parents? Was there ever a particular mistake or misstep made by either of your parents that served as a learning tool for you?

2. What is the greatest lesson learned in your adulthood that you would pass on to a young adult? Who stands out in your memory as your most profound mentor? Why? What part of your life has developed into the greatest area of positive personal evolution? What remains a growth area?

3. For women: If you had one pearl of wisdom to impart specifically to young men, what would it be? For men: If you had one pearl of wisdom to impart specifically to young women, what would it be? For all: What serves as your daily inspiration? Does faith play a part in that inspiration? Do you consider yourself a producer or a consumer? Why?

4. Do you agree with Mr. Sudler's decision to disassociate from his mother? Have you ever suffered from depression? Have you ever contemplated suicide? Is there a single most action of yours that you will always regret? What is the worst memory that you have? How did it personally affect you? What are some of the best memories that you hold dear?

5. What is your personal definition of a patriarch?